THE ART OF MANIPULATION

AN ESSENTIAL GUIDE TO LEARN PERSUASION AND DARK PSYCHOLOGY TECHNIQUES AND HOW TO STOP AND SPOT MANIPULATION ANALYZING PEOPLE

RAY BENEDICT

Tables of Contents

Introduction 4

What Is Manipulation 9

Manipulation In Depth 22

Types Of Manipulation 37

Deal With Manipulation 44

Causes Of Manipulation 51

How To Analyze And Manipulate People 62

Techniques Of Dark Psychology And Dark Manipulation 78

How To Talk 93

Conversational Skills Techniques 103

Secrets of Persuasive People, How to Stop And Spot Manipulation 116

Be A Positive Influence On Others 127

How To Defend Yourself From Manipulation 138

Conclusion 147

Introduction

Psychological warfare has been around for thousands of years. It has been used to instill fear in the enemy, create high or low morale, to intimidate, or even to inspire whole nations and mobilize soldiers. The best and effective kinds of psychological warfare is when the target doesn't even realize it. From Ancient civilizations to the Cold War, to the War on Terror. Psychological warfare has used techniques and tools based on the study of human behavior and thinking. The brain can be a powerful weapon and a weakness if properly manipulated both in and offensive and defensive way.

You may have also seen some techniques or practices a person in your life has used on you or others.

When looking over certain accounts of archetypical people who use certain techniques or practices, could you relate because you have used the same techniques? Maybe, you have realized that you may have been taken advantage of by someone who has used these techniques on you. If you feel surprised, excited or even guilty, you are not alone. Its purpose was to give you a rounded introduction into the realm of the study of dark psychology, techniques used in dark psychology, how to use some of these techniques and how to defend yourself for practitioners. It was only a taste of what dark psychology is.

Some of us have certain aspects of these skills or techniques ingrained in our lives and it has dictated our thoughts, actions and behaviors, we have in most cases readily used these skills from time to time. Some of us didn't realize that we are a "triangulator", "blaster", or a "projector", maybe even a "flirt". At the time we used some of the techniques. At the time, using them just seemed natural, as though it was instinctual. For some of us, these skills are as natural to us as breathing. Certain techniques may have become habitual through experiences in our environment, such as watching people close to us like a family member, friend or a significant other. Perhaps we saw a person we would consider a role model or a celebrity we admire use the exact same technique.

As human beings, we can have a need to feel a certain level of contentment. It is through this contentment that we can feel comfortable. We can feel this urge to find this contentment while at home, at school, or at work. When people, places or things impede on that contentment, we will react. Sometimes, we will learn from these situations or events on how to react the following time something impedes on our contentment again, either emotionally or methodically. Our behaviors and thoughts, as

well as how we react to them can be no different as how an animal reacts in the wild: A skunk, when feeling agitated, lifts its tail and shoots out an unpleasant liquid.

A bear will stand on its hind legs when it is ready to attack. For humans this is no difference.

You may have read about certain personality traits that use some of these dark psychological techniques, such as the narcissist or Machiavellian and related to some of their actions or behaviors.

 If you feel guilty or upset, please try not to feel bad. We may have behaviors that are triggered when certain current experiences have mirrored others from our past.

Some of our behaviors and reactions are natural to keep us safe such as recoiling from a hot stove or feeling slightly uneasy when we are on top of a building looking down. Others are learned and can be directly linked to our past.

It is up to us whether or not we want to make these thoughts or behaviors go away or reinforce them.

Suppose you would like to know how to use these techniques in your personal life for you own gain. We are ambitious by nature. Like was stated earlier, we all want to feel a sense of comfort and contentment in our world. Maybe you want more than what is considered enough for contentment. Envy and jealousy can be powerful motivational feelings. Suppose you may want to get into management at your office, want to build up your confidence in a conversation or debate, or maybe you want to attract that special someone you have had your eye on and want to get and keep their attention.

Maybe you really want to be the "alpha" and be feared and respected by your colleagues and friends. You may want to achieve your goals by any means.

As we have seen, the study of human psychology and the term "dark psychology" is very broad and has many interpretations about its areas of study.

The internet, much like any informative resource, comes with an almost subconscious "buyers beware" warning label. While there are many experienced and dedicated researchers, there are also people who claim to have working experience and have their own experiences and theories in dark psychology, particularly in manipulative and persuasive techniques. While everyone is certainly entitled to their own opinion and experience when it comes to this field of study, it is up to you, to form your own opinion and experiences should you choose to continue researching dark psychology.

What Is Manipulation

Manipulation is a form of social influence which uses indirect, underhanded, and deceptive tactics to change people's perceptions and their resultant behavior. Usually, the end goal is to advance the interests of the person who initiates the manipulation. In many cases, manipulation happens at the expense of the person that is being manipulated; they may be emotionally, mentally, or physically harmed, or they may end up taking actions that are against their own best interests.

It's important to note that social influence is not inherently bad; one person can use manipulation techniques for the good of the person he or she is manipulating. For example, your family members or friends can use social influence and manipulation to get you to do something for your own good. The people who mean you well might manipulate you as a way of helping you deal with certain challenges or to help you make the right decisions.

We are more interested in the kind of manipulation that is done with malicious intentions. This is the kind of manipulation that disregards a person's right to accept or reject influence. It is coercive in nature; when the person being targeted tries to push against it, this kind of manipulation gets more sophisticated, and the end goal is to negate the person's will to assert for themselves.

How Manipulation Works

There are several psychological theories that explain how successful manipulation works. The first and perhaps the most universally accepted theory is one that was put forth by renowned psychologist and author, George Simon. He analyzed the concept of manipulation from the point of view of the manipulator, and he can up with a pattern of behavior that sums up every manipulation scenario. According to Simon, there are three main things that are involved in psychological manipulation.

First, the manipulator approaches the target by concealing his or her aggressive intentions. Here, the manipulator seeks to endear himself to his target without revealing the fact that his ultimate plan is to manipulate him or her. The manipulator accomplishes this by modifying his behavior and presenting himself as a good-natured and friendly individual, one who relates well with the target.

Secondly, the manipulator will take time to know the victim. The purpose of this is to get to understand the psychological vulnerabilities that the victim may have so as to figure out which manipulation tactic will be the most effective when he ultimately decides to deploy them.

Depending on the scenario, and the complexity of the manipulation technique, this stage may take anywhere between a few minutes to several years. For example, when a stranger targets you, he may take only a couple of minutes to "size you up" but when your partner or colleague seeks to manipulate you, he or she may spend months or even years trying to understand how your mind works.

The success of this second step depends on how well the first step is executed. If the manipulator successfully hides his intentions from you, he is in a better position to learn your weaknesses because you will instill some level of trust in him, and he will use that trust to get you to let down your guard and to reveal your vulnerabilities to him.

Thirdly, having collected enough information to act upon, the manipulator will deploy a manipulation technique of his choosing. For this to work, the manipulator needs to be able to marshal a sufficient level of ruthlessness; this means that the manipulation technique chosen will depend on what the manipulator can stomach. A manipulator with a conscience may try to use methods that are less harmful to manipulate you. One that completely lacks a conscious may use extreme methods to take advantage of you. Either way, manipulative people are willing to let harm befall their victims, and to them, the resultant outcome (which is usually in their favor) justifies the harm they cause.

Simon's theory of manipulation teaches us the general approach that manipulators use to get what they want from their victims, but it also points out something extremely important: Manipulation works, not just because of the actions of the manipulator, but also because of the reactions of the victims.

In the first step, the manipulator misrepresents himself to the victim: If the victim is able to see through the veil that the manipulator is wearing, the manipulation won't be successful. In the second step, the manipulator collects information about victims to learn about his or her vulnerabilities. The victim can be may be able to stop the manipulation at this stage by treating the manipulator's prying nature with a bit of suspicion. In the third stage, the manipulator uses coercive or underhanded techniques to get what he wants from the victim. Even in this stage, the victim may have certain choices on how to react to the manipulator's machinations.

The point here is that when it comes to manipulation, it takes two to tango. By understanding both the victim's and the manipulator's psychology, it's possible to figure out how you can avoid falling victim to other people's manipulation, and it can also help you become more conscientious so that you don't unknowingly use manipulation techniques on other people around you.

Let's look at the vulnerabilities that manipulators like to exploit in their victims.

The first and most prevalent vulnerability is the need to please others. We all have this need to some extent; we seek to please the people in our lives as well as total strangers. This is technically a positive quality that helps us coexist in our societies, but to manipulators, it's a weapon that can be used against you.

Many of us are willing to endure certain levels of discomfort just to make other people feel happy; we feel a certain sense of obligation towards one another, and that's just human nature. The closer we are to certain people, the greater the need to please them. For example, the need to please your friend is higher than your need to please a stranger.

Manipulators understand this, and they use it against their victims all the time. If a manipulator wants to get something big out of you, he will first take the time to get closer to you, not just to get to know your vulnerability, but also to increase the sense of obligation you feel towards him.

The second vulnerability is the need for approval and acceptance. Again, as social beings, we all have an innate desire to feel accepted. We want people to love us, to think of us as members of their groups, and to choose us over other people. This feeling can be addictive, and it can give other people (especially manipulative ones) a lot of power over us. The vast majority of manipulation victims are people who have close personal relationships with the manipulators; in other words, they have an emotional need to gain the acceptance or approval of the manipulator. The remaining manipulation victims can be manipulated because they want to be a part of something (a group, a social class, etc.).

The third vulnerability that manipulators like to exploit is what psychologists refer to as "emetophobia" (which is the fear of negative emotions). To some extent, we are all afraid of negative emotions; we will do lots of things to avoid feeling angry, afraid, stressed, frustrated, and worried, etc. We want to lead happy and fulfilled lives, and anything that makes us feel "bad" is a threat to that sense of fulfillment. So, in many cases, we will do what manipulators want if it serves to alleviate that "bad" feeling. Manipulators know this, and they use negative emotions against us all the time.

The fourth vulnerability is the lack of assertiveness. Assertiveness is a very rare quality; even people who you may generally consider to be assertive are likely to cave in if manipulators push hard enough. Even when you are willing to stand your ground and to say "No," manipulators can be very persistent, and in the end, they can wear you out.

The fifth vulnerability is the lack of a strong sense of identity. Having a strong sense of identity means having clear personal boundaries, and understanding one's own values. Unfortunately, these qualities aren't so strong in most of us, and that leaves us open to manipulation. Manipulators succeed by pushing our boundaries little by little, making them blurry, and then taking control of our identities.

Finally, having an external locus of control, and having a low level of self-reliance are also key vulnerabilities that manipulators love to exploit. When you have an external locus of control, it means that your identity and your sense of self are external to you. It means you view yourself through other people's eyes. It means that you are extrinsically motivated. When you have low self-reliance, it means you depend on other people for sustenance and for emotional stability. It means that if support systems in your life are taken away, you can easily find yourself leaning on a manipulator, which leaves you at his mercy.

Manipulation is a Part of Human History

Looking at history, we will see that some of our most loved historical figures practiced manipulation. During the founding of the United States, our founding fathers had to use socio-political manipulation to help set a revolution in motion. By first using various economic manipulation tactics on the other colonies and colonists that joining their cause would benefit them more than say the British. Secondly, among each other many political games had to be played, all using subterfuge and manipulation to help get the right people in place to lead the country.

Manipulation had to be used in its persuasive form here so that the right person could get the right backing. This was not evil nor bad; it showed how the covert tactic of playing into a willing pawns card could allow for everyone involved to win. Imagine, too, that they had to manipulate the British for quite a while before things truly were sent into emotion. They had to manipulate them into trusting and believing them. These same kinds of manipulative games have been used for good by many great figures in history to simply manipulate their opposition into doing what is right.

Think of the rallies and marches during the civil rights movement. It did so much good by manipulating and playing on people's emotions and wants for a just society. This is not malicious manipulation, but more so an evil required to enact great change in this world.

Knowing that manipulation is not always an evil wantonly committed for evil makes it much easier to understand the kind of tactics people will use. In a big part complimenting and persuading someone through charisma is, in a sense, manipulation. You are telling them what they want to hear whether it compliments or being a shoulder to cry on for someone.

Almost every friendship that is healthy has this give and take. For a large part, these are simple altruistic forms of manipulation that allow and help both sides win and accomplish a goal of theirs. Charisma and persuasion two topics I mentioned earlier. Persuasion and charisma are the simplest forms of human manipulation.

Manipulators work by making someone come across as if they are the type of person who loves and cares about you and would drop anything if need be to help you with something. This glib or charm is a manipulative tactic that one could use for themselves to try and gain friends. Once again, there is nothing wrong with this; its more in line with gaming the system. You are putting on a front that people want, and as a result of this, they then become drawn to you easier and wish to spend time with you or do stuff to you.

This is a simple day to day manipulation that we all do – whether we realize it or not. This type of manipulation on a social scale is not for harm, but for companionship. Have you ever heard the expression "a little white lie"?

The issue is that the word makes manipulation sound bad and evil. But the truth is that by doing simple things that social charmer does, like mirroring body language, buying someone food, or always asking about their interests and ignoring yours is basic human interaction. You can get people to trust you and even help you get ahead in life, especially if this kind of interaction is taking place in the social world.

Manipulation and Success

You could argue that to a certain degree without some powerful people in society who used manipulation to get their way to the top, the world would fall apart. Maybe we would not be so successful. This kind of manipulation is far more different than the much more sinister mind manipulation. It is simple to understand the term mental manipulation. Simply put, mental manipulation occurs with the nefarious act of playing mind games, such as making you feel guilty for not buying or doing something, getting you to question your own judgment.

This covert manipulative behavior can become so common that we oftentimes don't recognize it until it is too late by which point, we have befallen the consequences of said manipulation. Avoiding these consequences is a great thing to be capable of doing. But it can be hard to avoid if you are not sure what you are avoiding. Well, that is why it is good to know what mental manipulation is due to its subtlety. It is this type of manipulation – mental manipulation – which is perhaps the most common form of manipulation you will encounter in your day to day life.

Mental manipulation shows its face a lot in relationships with friends or other people you care about. As a result, the people who do this are very good at it and hide it well. Besides being such a common form of manipulation people will use, it is important to realize that there are many varieties of mental manipulation to which you could easily find yourself as a victim.

Consider times when you are speaking with a group of friends, and one person tries to make you feel guilty due to you making a choice to not buy them an extremely expensive gift for their birthday. They then might try mental manipulation to get you to fall for the trap of "oh well, I have done all these things for you; do you not think it is fair if you get me xyz."

Behavior like this is where manipulation becomes evil and unacceptable. This is not trying to sway someone over to your side of thinking for a good reason or trying to survive in a time of crisis. This narcissistic person is using manipulation to hurt people, and that is never acceptable.

Understanding the subtle moral differences in manipulation makes it easier for you to appreciate how to learn about different manipulative tactics as a whole and how you yourself can go about defending from and using them as well as giving you the useful ability of knowing how to avoid people who could potentially try and manipulate you in person, this includes the media and everything else we see. Since they all use manipulation tactics, understanding this is half the battle.

Manipulation In Depth

How would you feel if you never realized that all along you had been used as a pawn? Or that you've been acting out someone else's script? The realization that you have never been entirely in charge of your life or actions, in general, can crush you. It sounds scary. This is essentially what emotional manipulation is about. People usually toss the word emotional manipulation in regular conversations, but they seldom know what it truly means. Thus, it is quite essential to understand what emotional manipulation entails and to set the record straight. Emotional manipulation is a psychological or social means by which an individual who might be wise, or at least thinks he is, influences your behavior or responses to a situation or issue in a manner that isn't true to yourself intending to satisfy his needs or wants.

You might think you're still yourself because you don't realize you're acting out someone else's script. Their approach doesn't always have to be forceful, but it certainly plays your psyche to their beat. Manipulation is exploitative and can cripple you with self-doubt. It is about someone else using what truly covertly belongs to you to fulfill all their desires without obtaining your permission to do so. The main issue isn't about the secrecy involved, but about the fact that manipulators can make you do things you might have not commonly done.

Tactics of Covert Manipulation

A lot of people are unaware of the fact that manipulators are continually trying to confuse and control them. You might have experienced a feeling of uneasiness because the manipulator's words don't match his actions, or you might feel like you're being forced to accept a specific request even though it feels like a demand. The way people react usually tends to escalate the degree of abuse and essentially encourages them to play into the hands of the manipulator. All this can make the person being manipulated start to feel guilty or even small.

If you're dealing with a manipulator, then the phrase, "know your enemy" is something you must be aware of. You must be able to spot any red flags and respond strategically to the covert tactics of manipulation. By understanding what the manipulator is up to, it puts you in a better position to protect yourself. You cannot defend yourself if you're not aware of what is happening. If someone is behaving passive-aggressively towards you, it is known as covert aggression. The extent of consciousness or unconsciousness of a manipulator's behavior is debatable. From a victim's perspective, it never matters, because the effect happens to be the same. If you display any empathy towards the manipulator, it is the risk of being mistreated in the future increases drastically. Regardless of whether the manipulator's attack on you is overt or covert, it is known as aggression.

If you are unaware of the tactics which manipulators use, it will be quite challenging to break free from their spell or hold over you. You may be deceiving yourself that you are in charge of your life and actions, even when you are not. Emotional manipulation is often seen in a bad light, but there are times when you might need to use it to get what you need from individuals who wouldn't cooperate with you initially. By being aware of the various tactics of manipulation, you cannot only prevent yourself from being manipulated but can also take corrective action if you're being manipulated. Emotional manipulators often work on the weak points in the victim's psyche and use the same to make themselves feel better.

It is a widespread belief that most of the covert manipulators say or do things intentionally to get whatever they desire. The two things a covert manipulator wants more than anything else are power and control. The apparent goal of any form of manipulation is to influence others to meet one's needs. However, chronic manipulators often do this to get control and power over others. They maintain their domination over others through constant and recurring emotional manipulation and emotional abuse. They are often passive-aggressive and might lie, act like the injured party or even pretend surprise if you complain about their behavior. Any criticism aimed towards them can be easily turned against you. If you are wondering why a manipulator acts the way he does, then you aren't alone. They usually do this for the following reasons.

- To make your defensive or to lower your guard

- To avoid any form of confrontation

- To trigger self-doubt in their target

- To make you question your judgment along with your perception of reality

- To brush away any responsibility

- To hide their manipulative nature or ulterior motives

- To avoid changing their behavior

Being subjected to manipulation can make you lose your trust in yourself and have you doubting everything you feel and perceive. Some forms of aggression, like blatant criticism and narcissistic abuse, are quite common. However, there are other subtle forms of emotional manipulation or abuse like complaining, denial, feigning ignorance, shifting blame, lying, emotional blackmail, and insincere flattery which are less noticeable. The techniques employed by emotional predators are varied and numerous.

Lying

A habitual liar is someone who is used to lying all the time, even when it isn't required. They don't lie because they are guilty or afraid, but they do this intending to try to confuse you. By confusing you, they take away your ability to make rational decisions and making you easy to manipulate to get what they want. Some manipulators use accusations along with other manipulative tactics to make you defensive. Lying doesn't always have to be direct. Indirect means of lie include the omission of specific information or providing vague information.

Absolute denial

Lying and denial tend to go hand in hand. The tactic of denial used by emotional predators is not unconscious, unlike the one where the victims of abuse don't realize they are being abused. Another example of unconscious denial is an addict who doesn't know he has an addiction. Whenever an emotional predator employs denial, he is quickly disavowing any promises he has made or denying the knowledge about such signs, behavior, or even arguments. The manipulator might also try to minimize and rationalize his behavior by coming up with excuses. Don't be surprised if the manipulator attempts to make it seem like you're making a big deal out of a tiny issue or tries to rationalize his actions by making you question your judgment. He might even come up with various excuses to gain your sympathy. Once you give in, you are sinking deeper into his manipulative trap.

Avoid confrontations

A manipulator never likes to accept his faults or shoulder his responsibilities. He doesn't like taking responsibility for his actions or words. He will try to avoid confrontation at all costs. If you notice that someone is continuously avoiding any discussions about their behavior or is refusing to discuss it, it is a tactic of manipulation. Not only will he avoid a confrontation, but he will also try shifting the blame onto you. Since a manipulator knows he can control you, the possibility of an encounter can prompt a response like "stop harping on me," "don't be such a nag," or "you are a fault-finding machine." Mostly the manipulator is trying to shift the blame onto you. Avoidance doesn't always have to be apparent; it can be subtle. A manipulator can subtly change the topic of discussion to take the spotlight away from himself. Or he might try flattering you or giving you compliments to take the focus away from the issue. Emotional abusers might say things like, "You know how much I love you," to lower your defenses. Once he succeeds, you might not even remember why you were upset to begin with.

By being evasive, an emotional predator blurs the facts and confuses you by planting seeds of self-doubt. A manipulator becomes slightly uncomfortable when you point out any inconsistencies in his stories and might even claim that you aren't compatible together. A skilled manipulative liar hates it when others question his stories and half-truths. In fact, he might quickly shift the blame onto you and make you doubt your judgment.

Shame and guilt

Another common tactic employed by emotional predators is projection. It's a defensive tactic wherein the manipulator starts accusing others of his actions or behaviors. Remember the saying, "the best defense is a great offense?" Well, the manipulator is primarily using this tactic by shifting the blame onto his victim. By doing this, he is putting you on the defensive. The manipulator shrugs off any responsibility for his actions and stays innocent while you are now left to deal with any shame or guilt you experience. A manipulator is fully aware of his victim's style of thinking and will use this knowledge against the victim. An abuser will come up with ways to blame others and his victims instead of apologizing for his behavior. This is quite similar to the way a criminal uses a defense of police incompetence to shift the blame onto others. A partner who is aggressive and resorts to physical violence might blame his spouse for his behavior. By moving the responsibility onto others and making their victims feel guilty, they are gaining control and power over the victim.

By guilt-tripping you and shaming you, he is essentially gaining power over you. So, the worse you feel, the better it is for the manipulator. He might even act like a martyr and say he deserves better after all that he has done for you. This can be coupled with harsh criticism that you are ungrateful or even selfish. Shaming is not just about making you feel guilty, but it is also about triggering feelings of inadequacy. By demeaning you, he is making himself feel better. For instance, a manipulator will effectively shift the blame onto his victims by suggesting everything is their fault and not his. For example, "we would have had a happy relationship if you would just believe me and stop being paranoid." At times, spouses might compare their existing relationship with a prior connection to make their current partner feel inferior and weak.

The best way to blame the victim is by using guilt and shame. For instance, even if you find concrete evidence on your partner's phone, suggesting that he's cheating on you, the manipulator will find a way to turn this against you. Instead of coming clean about his indiscretion, he might act like you are violating his privacy or that you had no right to check his phone. He might also act like the victim or say you don't trust him. He is essentially taking away the focus from his indiscretion and is now concentrating on your actions by blaming you; your partner has successfully avoided a confrontation about his cheating. In the end, you, the actual victim in the situation, will start to feel guilty about your actions. You might also feel like your anger is no longer justified or valid. He is invalidating your feelings while getting away with his misdeeds.

Intimidation

Intimidation can be mental as well as physical and doesn't always come in the form of direct threats. It can also be in the form of statements like, "I am well-connected and have friends in high places," "you aren't as young as you once were," or "have you considered the consequences of your decision?" Another strategy commonly employed by manipulators is to come up with fictitious stories told to provoke fear in their victims. A manipulator uses his victim's anxiety to get what he desires - a sense of absolute control.

Magnification

While dealing with a manipulator, he will often magnify his problems while diminishing the intensity of your questions. This is usually done quite subtly so that you don't even realize that you're being manipulated. For instance, if you bring up a problem with any trauma you faced in childhood, a manipulative partner will point out that he never even had parents to begin with. Initially, it might seem like the manipulator is sympathizing with you, but effectively he is just diminishing your problems. By doing this, he is trying to make you feel like your problems are not worth pondering over or even discussing.

Aggressive jokes

It might seem like the manipulator is joking, but here's sneakily engaging in offensive jokes which demean you as a person. Often, the manipulator will joke about any insecurities you have or any issues you are struggling with. This is done to overpower you. Don't be surprised if the manipulator or partner starts joking about any trauma you suffered in life. For instance, joking about a failed marriage is not funny, but this doesn't prevent the manipulator from doing so. Mostly, he is trying to hurt you but is doing so by masquerading the insult in the form of a joke or sarcasm. So, if you do react towards it, you will come across as being extremely touchy about an issue, which he must not have even joked about, to begin with.

Name-calling

A manipulator often believes that he is right when others are always wrong. He will go to any extent to prove that he is right. If you're not thick-skinned, then you cannot deal with the kind of criticism a manipulator doles out. You can feel quite annoyed and even rejected once someone starts calling you an extremist, a troublemaker, or even an idiot. A manipulator will resort to name-calling to overpower you. Once you begin to feel bad about yourself, you become incredibly vulnerable to manipulation.

Smear campaign

Gossiping and indulging in smear campaigns are two things a manipulator will never shy away from. Gossip can be quite harmful when left unchecked. It is not beneath a manipulator to spread vicious rumors about you. He does all this to make others think ill about you. All the vile stories he covers will undoubtedly harm your equation with others.

Triangulation

In this technique, the manipulator will try to validate his wrongdoings or wrong acts towards you by making you question someone else instead of the manipulator himself. The manipulator might be mentally abusive towards you and the moment you react to it by letting him know that such behavior isn't acceptable to you, they will conveniently direct your attention to what someone else is doing. For instance, if you complain about the mistreatment he's doling out, he might point out that another friend of yours is perfectly fine when her partner mistreats her. By doing this, he is distracting you while making you feel like you're overreacting.

All these tactics can cripple your self-confidence and kill your identity as an individual. You can forgive and move on, but never forget. If you turn a blind eye toward it, the manipulation will continue. After a while, you will be riddled with trauma, and your self-worth will take a massive blow. The first step to dealing with manipulation is to become aware of the problem.

Why Is Manipulation Undesirable

Perhaps the most apparent reason why manipulation is considered to be genuinely undesirable is that it is morally wrong. Apart from this, it also harms the person being manipulated. This harm can be emotional, mental, or even physical at times. For instance, an advertisement glorifying the purchase and use of cigarettes is manipulative. It is worshiping something, which is detrimental to one's health. Manipulation uses tactics that are usually considered to be immoral or, at best, dodgy. It is quintessential that we all treat one another as rational beings instead of objects to be played with. Manipulation is often carried on to gain undue advantage over others to fulfill the needs of the manipulator. Therefore, it is safe to say that manipulation is selfish. Various tactics employed by the manipulator tend to take away the victim's freedom to choose. So, essentially, the manipulator is forcing his victims to do something, regardless of whether they want to or not. Manipulation is also quite similar to lying. The manipulator is always in control of his victim's behavior and thinking. Manipulation can also harm the victim's sense of self, self-esteem, and self-confidence.

Types of Manipulators

There are different types of manipulators, and each of them tends to use a specific technique to manipulate their targets.

Perhaps the most common type of manipulator you will ever come across is the one who makes you feel guilty. Nothing can make you feel worse than an unnecessary guilt trip. If you don't comply with the demands of the manipulator, he will make you feel guilty about it. Even if it were right to deny his claim, the manipulator would do everything he possibly can to make you feel bad.

A masked braggart tends to make his target feel inferior or inadequate covertly. These kinds of manipulators are well aware of the fact that he will look proud and presumptuous, not to mention arrogant if he always brags about his accomplishments. He is worried that others will think of him as being bold. However, he indeed loves bragging about his accomplishments, and he goes about doing this differently. For instance, this kind of manipulator will never call his victim fat, but will instead say, "My small size shirts are so baggy now," even when he knows his victim wears XL. By belittling his victim, he is boasting about his accomplishments.

Types Of Manipulation

Many of us are aware that manipulation is a form of deceit. Manipulators are the people who use deceptive tactics to achieve what they want, but this is regardless of the consequences to those around them, particularly to the victims of their tactics.

Manipulators are not worried about how their manipulation will affect you personally or psychological damage that they inflict; all they care about is getting the results that they want. These results could be anything from getting to pick the restaurant to getting access to the funds or gifts needed to perpetuate a particular social standing.

Knowing the warning signs is a start, but knowing the type of emotional manipulator you are dealing with can also help you in defending yourself against them and their deceptive tactics. So let's talk about the various types of manipulators out in the world, thus gaining a more complete understanding of how they operate to achieve their ends.

Indifferent

First up is the indifferent manipulator, which is the one that acts like they don't care. These manipulators often seem indifferent towards anything you are doing or saying. This indifference is not just toward your actions, but any circumstances in your life, including difficulties or even celebrations.

In acting indifferent, these individuals have actually caught your attention. You spend time and energy attempting to achieve that breakthrough to capture their attention, thus hoping to achieve a deeper connection. However, they have already singled you out for some specific reason, so they will provide just enough interest to keep you hooked without really breaking out of the indifferent cycle.

In fact, the more indifferent they act, the more questions you are going to ask because you genuinely care. However, when you start asking questions that is when the manipulation starts in an earnest fashion, because now a manipulator can use that they have information provided through those conversations to dig their hooks in ever deeper. Without them having to do or say anything directly, they have begun to play on your heart strings, thus achieving the goal of your personal emotional investment into their lives.

As the victim, you are now in a position that allows them to use your sympathy to "make them feel better", but in reality, the manipulator is now just starting their sting to take from their victims whatever they want, from the emotional to the material. But when the victim has nothing left, then the manipulator moves on to their following victim, typically without any real remorse.

Still at this moment, you are still a goose to be fleeced, so the indifferent manipulator may also take advantage of another type of manipulator, which is the one that is always in distress or poor me.

Poor Me

This particular type of manipulator may be the easiest to spot, but in combination with other traits, makes them easy to fall for over and over again. So, what do the poor me manipulators do so effectively when dealing with their victims?

The poor me manipulators use sympathy and guilt, appealing to their victims need to try to help another human being in trouble or assist someone out of a sense of charity or faith. Appealing to their victim's better nature is one consistent way that a manipulator will attempt to get into someone's head. Often it is this goodness that a manipulator can turn on their victim.

It is simply part of our human nature to feel for people who are struggling through something or who are facing various challenges different from the ones that we are facing. We react by doing what we can to help them out, so we tend to cater to their demands without realizing we are being manipulated.

The demands can at first appear reasonable, but over time, will simply grow in complexity. These requests quickly turn into commands and ones that often prove to be real time suckers. Thus, your whole world suddenly becomes completely focused on the manipulator. So the isolation can begin, making it harder for you or loved ones to observe the manipulation and point it out to you.

Critic

As with other manipulators, this particular type is a bit more aggressive than the first two types. They will actively focus on their victim's habits and emotional cues. After finding areas of sensitivity or weakness, the manipulator will begin to focus on them, subtlety at first, and then gradually growing bolder over time.

While it might be easy to spot what a manipulator is doing, many of us who fall victim to manipulators are helpless to stop it, unless we work on improving our mindset. Other ways to help avoid being a victim or getting out of a manipulative situation involve using anti-manipulation techniques.

The critic uses criticism as a way to get what they want because the victim is trying to please, although the critical manipulator will set a bar for their standards, which the victim will find impossible to meet. The constant criticism for their victim contributes to neither making them feel like they are not good enough nor will they ever be good enough. Through manipulation the critic makes you feel like you are worthless and they are better than you.

Thus, to achieve a better sense of your own self-worth, the victim will attempt to be more like the critic or to do things just the way the critic prefers them. Personality changes may also occur, because the victim just wants to gain the affection and praise of the critic. However, the victim does not know this goal is simply unachievable.

Still as bad as these types of manipulators can prove to be, there is one that can be far worse. Why? Because they are willing to go much further than any of the others to achieve their goals, including using fear and violence.

Intimidators

When this particular manipulator comes into play, the victim can be in a very dangerous place. These manipulators are the worst of the worst; they are even more aggressive than the critic. In fact, the intimidator is not just critical, but they use fear and violence to make their victims cower.

These manipulators are more familiar with the stick, than using a more carrot like approach. Once their victim is afraid, these manipulators can easily have their demands met. In abusive relationships with intimidators, the tactic of using anger comes out frequently, along with the need to punish. Both of these tactics play into the fear aspect of the intimidator.

Let's face it, when we are afraid of someone, as individuals we tend to give in much quicker than if we felt in a position of power or a defendable position. These manipulators are all about stripping away any sense of being able to defend yourself, physically or psychologically.

Nobody dares stand up to a person who uses fear to manipulate them because they are literally afraid of what that person might physically do. This is where the manipulator uses violence or the threat of violence to complete their hold on the victim. Abusive spousal relationships often demonstrate this type of intimidation manipulation with a mix of violence all too well.

So now that we have a greater understanding of the manipulator, their types and tactics, it's time to get a better understanding of the victim. However, you might be the one displaying those traits.

So what specifically about your personality or way of carrying yourself is sending up flags for a manipulator to zero in on?

Deal With Manipulation

Psychological manipulation is always going to be a very loaded and heavy-handed issue. It can often be referred to as lying, deceiving, skewing, distorting, gaslighting, intimidating, guilting, and other such things. Manipulators can also take the form of many different people over the course of your life. Sometimes, the person who is manipulating you might be a parent, sibling, boss, classmate, coworker or romantic partner, among others. That's why manipulation is such a complex topic to handle. It can take the form of various tactics, and it can also be employed by various agents. This is why it can be increasingly difficult for someone to be able to identify and deal with a manipulative person.

You were exposed to the many different feelings, sensations, and experiences that you might have should you ever find yourself in a manipulative relationship environment. As long as you keep your eyes peeled and you make an active effort in seeking these red flags out, it shouldn't really be a problem. Now, it's a matter of dealing with these people and managing their advances.

First evaluate whether the person is more of a systematic or unconscious manipulator. The more systematic, profound manipulators are almost certainly beyond reach. They can have grand visions and don't care who they have to get by to pursue their goals, they may simply enjoy controlling others, perhaps they have had childhood traumas and issues that lead them to exploit others for fulfillment. These types of people are more aware of it and aggressively pursue their manipulative traits. Whatever the case may be, if possible, keep your distance on these types of people. Indeed, the easy solution would be to cut this person out of your life, right? It can be so easy to just burn bridges with someone if you know that they have manipulative tendencies and that they would be so willing to advance their own personal interests at your expense. That kind of selfishness should warrant a cutting of ties. However, it's not always going to be that simple. There are going to be times when the person who is manipulating you is someone you have a deep bond and connection with. There is even a chance they are not consciously aware of their behavior themselves. For instance, if your parent, partner or friend is manipulating you, it's not going to be so easy to just break that relationship off entirely. This is especially true if you love your parents and you know that they love you in return. In this case, it's not just a matter of eliminating a manipulative person from your life. Rather, it becomes an issue of managing this individual.

When dealing with a manipulative person, it's very important that you tread lightly. Keep in mind that there is also a paternal kind of manipulation. They might not have bad intentions, and they might take offense to the fact that you are accusing them of being manipulative. That is why you have to be extra cautious and sensitive when you broach the issue with them.

First, Be Safe

If you know that you are in danger whenever you are with this manipulative individual in your life, always make sure that there is a third-party present. You can never really know what they might do to you if the two of you are alone. So, before you confront them about your manipulation, make sure that you have someone else in the room. You need that mediator; someone who would be able to help bridge the two of you. You can always call on a mutual friend, a shared loved one, or a trusted confidante. In more serious cases, you can even seek professional help from a licensed therapist. The point here is that the confrontation process should never be conducted recklessly. Your safety is always going to be the first priority here. And a lot of the time, that means having someone else in the room to be with you.

Take a Diplomatic Approach to Initiating a Dialogue

You can either choose to work your own influence on them to lessen the negative effects, or you could just confront them. The initial confrontation doesn't have to be so hot and impassioned. In fact, the best approach to confronting this individual would be to be as calm and collected as can be. You want to make sure that you are taking emotions out of the equation here. Keep in mind that a manipulative person is always going to capitalize on the emotionality of a person. If you take that ammo away from them, then it leaves them very little to work with. In addition to that, it's more likely that they won't react in such a hostile manner if you take a more civil approach to initiating this dialogue with them. Using people's own words against them makes it harder to resist whatever it is you are asking them to do, if one claims to be selfless, then they would not partake in certain actions to begin with.

You have to remember that starting the conversation

isn't always going to go so smoothly. It's very much likely that they will resist at first. However, you need to stay persistent. You have to emphasize the importance of this conversation. However, if they do decide to engage with you in this conversation, then you need to stay mindful of the following tips.

Don't Fight Back

If they are going to be hostile with you about it, resist the urge to fight back. You have to learn to pick your spots. Responding to them in a hostile manner is only going to result in you playing into their games. You don't want that. You want to make sure that you stay calm all throughout. When they get emotional, don't invalidate these feelings. Their emotions might actually be very authentic regardless of whether they are based on distorted truths or not. A person can still feel angry about something that is a complete lie or fantasy. Keep that in mind.

Instead of invalidating their feelings and telling them that they're being unreasonable, hear them out. With this method, you will get a chance to really understand them more. You will be able to gain insight into their behavioral triggers. The more you understand them, then the better it will be for you to manage this entire situation.

Set Clear Limits and Boundaries

Once you have heard their side of the tale, it's now time for you to air out your personal grievances. Again, you need to make sure that you keep emotions out of it. You don't want them to be invalidating what you're saying just because you're being hysterical. You want to be honest about it, and be straight. You shouldn't be beating around the bush anymore. Make sure that all of the skeletons come out of the closet. Be courteous, but also, don't pull any punches. No matter how uncomfortable it might be to speak honestly about your feelings, you're going to have to do so.

If you're interested in salvaging the relationship, then emphasize this point. Make sure they understand that you don't want to block them out of your life completely. However, you also need to emphasize that you will be setting clear limits and boundaries as you move forward in your relationship together. Make them understand that the integrity of your relationship is dependent on their respect for the boundaries that you set in it.

Know When It's Time to Walk Away

Sometimes, you just need to be able to know when it's

time to walk away. No matter how painful it is to cut yourself loose from someone who you love dearly, you still have to do so for the sake of your own well-being. You should not be making any room for toxicity or manipulative behavior that causes burden in your life regardless of who it might be coming from. At the end of the day, the only real person who has your back is yourself. That is why you have to make it a point to protect yourself at all costs. If there is no way for you to find a peaceful means of coexisting with one another that doesn't involve any form of harmful manipulation that is taking value out of your life, then you need to be able to walk away from that.

Granted, walking away from someone who is close to you isn't going to be a quick and easy process. It's going to be a very painful and gradual one. However, you always need to prioritize your own well-being above the relationships that you have with others, especially if they are the toxic and systematic type. Stay safe and guarded. No relationship is worth losing your sense of self over.

Causes Of Manipulation

Now that you are fairly competent in identifying emotional and covert manipulation tactics, let's understand what leads people to manipulate others. This may help you deal with them more efficiently.

We've all been victims of everything from pathological lying to being made to feel inadequate to suffering awful smear campaigns. They are beyond reasonable standards of human behavior. What makes people turn into sinister manipulators? What leads manipulators to use the tactics they do? What makes them defy norms of human behavior and turn to underhanded techniques to have their way with people?

Read on to get deeper insights about what makes people manipulate others in ways you'd never imagine.

Fear

Why does a person use manipulation to fulfill his/her own agenda? Simple - fear!

It is obvious that manipulators fear that they will never be able to gain the desired outcome on their own abilities.

That if they act ethically, people and life will not reward them positively. They operate from the view that people are life, and people are positioned against them. Manipulators fear everyone as their enemy and believe life will not necessarily be favorable to them if they act favorably.

There is a fear that resources are limited, and if they don't gain something, others will. They think it's a dog-eat-dog universe where people must be controlled to help them accomplish the desired result. This control can be in any form – emotional, psychological, financial or practical. They want to control people, so they can achieve their desired agenda and put their fear to rest.

Manipulators are constantly living under fear and insecurity. 'What if this doesn't happen?' 'What if my partner leaves me for someone else?' 'What if someone gains an upper hand over me?' They want to win and control all the time to combat an inherent sense of fear.

Where does this fear stem from? It originates from a deep sense of unworthiness. This simply translates as 'I am certainly not worthy of the good things and people in life, hence, these things and people will leave me. To prevent them from leaving me, I must resort to some underhanded techniques that will give me absolute control over the people and things I believe I don't deserve.' In short, the underlying message is – 'I am undeserving or unworthy of people and things!'

Low or No Conscience

Lack of conscience is another fundamental reason for manipulation. When a person fails to realize that he/she is responsible for their own reality, there is a greater tendency to operate without a conscience. Manipulators don't believe a fair system exists. Also, they've stopped evolving. They don't learn from earlier experiences or try to accomplish a state of congruence between inner emotions and external life.

They view manipulation as a safe or secure world for getting the desired result, despite the fact that these results have not brought them satisfaction in the past. Emotionally and psychologically, they keep coming back to square one from time to time, never learning their lesson. To avoid this lesson, they will create another reason to manipulate. Thus, they are caught in vicious circle of unworthiness or dissatisfaction, thus, creating another manipulation need.

Manipulation doesn't pay beyond the initial brief fix since the manipulative action is not authentic, balanced or effective. It is a defense reaction to perceived hurt, unworthiness, fear or insecurity. By being manipulative, the person is attempting to offset these emotions.

Manipulation is a deliberate act that is not aligned with a person's conscience or greater good. The person doesn't operate with a "we are one" understanding, which means he/she seeks to gain through manipulation by authenticity rather than non-authenticity. Anything gained through non-authenticity only leads to narrow victories, ongoing trouble, emptiness or fear and unworthiness. This creates an even bigger sense of unworthiness. Again, unworthiness is a fear of not being worthy of others' love and acceptance.

Manipulative folks do not learn, evolve or realize the power of authenticity. Lack of realization of the real power of authenticity and worthiness comes from knowing that one is cherished and accepted for what they really are. In essence, a feeling of unworthiness is often at the core of manipulation.

They Don't Want to Pay the Price Attached to Reach Their

Goals

People often manipulate to serve their needs because they do not want to pay the price attached to their goal. They often strive to accomplish the objective or serve their purpose without wanting to give back or pay the price in return.

For instance, if you don't want your partner to leave you, the relationship will take work. You'll have to give your partner love, compassion, understanding, time, loyalty, encouragement, inspiration, a secure future and much more.

A manipulator may not want his/her partner to leave them, but they don't want to pay the price of maintaining a happy, secure and healthy relationship, whereby the partner will never leave them. They may not want to be loyal or spend much time with their partner, and yet they expect them to stay. When people are not ready to pay the price of accomplishing what they want, they may resort to manipulation or underhanded techniques to achieve these goals without paying the price attached to them.

Similarly, if a manipulative person wants to be promoted in his/her workplace, rather than working hard, staying past work hours, upgrading their skills or getting a degree, they will simply manipulate their way into the position. The person is not prepared to pay the price or do what it takes to be promoted.

At times, it's deeply ingrained in a person's psyche that wants are bad or that he/she shouldn't have any desires since it makes them come across as selfish. Manipulation then becomes a way to get what they desire or need without even asking for it.

Manipulators realize there is a price attached to everything. A person won't do them a favor without expecting a favor in return. They won't keep getting things if they don't demonstrate kindness and gratitude. A person won't love them or have sex with them without getting commitment, loyalty and love in return. Manipulators try to push their luck by trying to get something without paying the price attached to it. It is often the easy way out.

They Think They Won't Get Caught

Another reason people manipulate is because they think they can get away with their sneaky acts and that the victims won't realize they are being manipulated. They are also confident that the victim can't do anything even if their manipulation cover is blown.

What gives manipulators the feeling that they won't be caught? Some people come across as inherently clueless, vulnerable, insecure and naïve. These are the type of people manipulators prey on. They believe a person who has low confidence, a low sense of self-worth or is clueless about the ways of the world is less likely to figure out that he/she is being manipulated.

Also, manipulators know that in the event that their manipulation cover is blown, the victim will not be able to do much. They cleverly pick targets who are low in confidence, self-acceptance, body image or sense of self-worth. It is easier to play on the vulnerabilities of these people than on assertive and self-assured people who won't allow people to take advantage of them.

For example, say a person has low awareness of social dynamics, doesn't understand jokes easily, doesn't identify a prank early, is unable to differentiate between genuine courtesy and sexual advances, can't tell when someone is genuinely attracted to them or simply wants to go to bed with them and other similar social and interpersonal dynamics. That person is more likely to be manipulated.

Manipulators are well aware that their victims can't do anything if they don't even realize that their weaknesses are being misused. They often cash in on the cluelessness of their victims by saying they are imagining things or making something up. An already clueless and unsure person is less likely to question this idea. When you are already reeling under feelings of insecurity, cluelessness and vulnerability, how difficult is it for a manipulator to take advantage of these feelings by reinforcing them further?

Manipulators

Manipulators manipulate because they think they can hurt or upset their victims more than the victims can hurt or upset them. They will almost always target people who come across as nice and vulnerable. When people are oblivious to the dishonesty existing within social relationships, they aren't really accustomed to dishonest allegiances. This doesn't equip them with the means to confront or counter dishonesty, which makes them less aware of being manipulated.

They Aren't Able to Accept Their Shortcomings

When people are unable to come to terms with their shortcomings or do not accept the responsibility or accountability for their faults, there is an inherent need to make others feel lesser than them.

If manipulators aren't good enough or feel miserable about themselves, there is a desire to make others feel equally worthless or miserable about themselves. When a person believes he/she is unworthy of someone, they will manipulate the person to feel unworthy, too. They can then gain control over his/her perception that they need the manipulator in their life to feel worthy. By putting others down or gaining control over others, they experience a form of pseudo superiority. If they can't be good enough for others, they make others feel like they aren't good enough to retain control over them.

In effect, manipulators don't want their victims to realize that they (the manipulators) aren't good enough or unworthy of them (the victims). The manipulator will therefore carefully cultivate a feeling of helplessness and unworthiness within the victim to keep them hooked to him/her. If a person realizes that he/she is more attractive, intelligent, richer, capable, efficient, self-sufficient etc., the higher their chances will be of leaving the manipulator. On the other hand, if the manipulator injects a feeling of the person not being 'complete,' they'll need someone to 'complete' them.

Manipulators are not able to accept their shortcomings or deal with criticism. They are often grappling with deep psychological issues or insecurities. By manipulating others, they do not have to confront their own insecurities to feel higher than others. For someone operating with such a narrow perspective, even a little correction, feedback or criticism can seem like a huge defeat.

People who manipulate don't know how to deal with defeat. When you hesitate to give feedback because the person will get defensive or blow things out of proportion or won't take things in the right spirit, it may be a sign you are dealing with someone who can't come to terms with criticism.

Notice how manipulators will seldom express feelings of gratitude or thankfulness. They find it challenging to be grateful to others because, in their view, by doing so they are increasing their sense of being obligated to another person, which doesn't give them an upper hand in any relationship.

For example, if you do someone a huge favor, they feel obliged to return that favor, which puts you above them in the relationship dynamics until they return the favor. Manipulators don't want to give you the upper hand by feeling obliged to you. Therefore, they will demonstrate minimal gratefulness, so you don't believe you've done something huge for them or that they are obliged to you. The idea is to always be one-up on you, and this feeling of being indebted to you doesn't make them feel one-up.

How To Analyze And Manipulate People

As explored, there are many stimuli that trigger human responses and lead to decision-making, and researchers have developed extensive methods to measure these outcomes, whether using biometrics, surveys, or focus groups. However, these research methods may not be at your disposal on a daily basis. Below are methods techniques you can use in everyday interactions to analyze cognitive and behavioral processes of individuals around you.

Observe Body Language

Research found that body language accounts for 55% of how we communicate, while words only account for 7%. The tone of voice represents the rest. People can tend to be over-analytical when reading human behavior and it may seem counterintuitive, but in order to be objective in analyzing people, observe naturally and try not to over-analyze.

Appearance

One of the first things that speak the loudest is the appearance of an individual. Take notice of a person's dressing. Is he or she dressed sharply in a suit, traditional clothing, or casual style? Does he or she look particularly conscious about the choice of clothing or hairstyle? The way a person dresses can determine his or her level of self-esteem.

Posture

When reading people's posture, observe if they hold their head high or slouch. Do they walk indecisively or walk with a confident chest? How do they esteem themselves? Posture also reveals confidence levels or a person's physical pain points.

Movements

People generally lean towards things they like, and away from things they do not. Crossed arms and legs suggest self-protection, anger, or defensiveness. When people cross their legs, their toes point to the person they are most comfortable with, or away from those they are not. When hands are placed in pockets, laps, or behind the back, it is an indication that the person is hiding something. Nervousness can also be revealed through lip-biting or cuticle-picking. Some people do that to soothe themselves under pressure or in awkward situations.

Facial Expressions

Aforementioned, emotions may not be visible unless expressed. Frown lines indicate over-thinking or worry, while crow's feet evidence joyfulness. Tension, anger, or bitterness can be seen on pursed lips or clenched jaws. Facial expressions can be one of the most evident ways to read human behavior towards specific things, places, or people.

How to analyze people effectively and efficiently

So, you want to learn how to analyze people effectively and efficiently. Well, you came to the right place! I will teach you everything you need to know about reading others. I will even teach you how to understand yourself. We need to talk about a few things before we get into the meat of the matter, however.

There are so many different methods to analyze others, and it can be hard to pick it all apart. Where did this practice come from? Why is it important to understand how to analyze others?

As it turns out, the art of analyzing others has existed

since–well, we had the intelligence to do it. Human beings are, by nature, herd animals. We are highly in tune with others, and our lives are driven by societal expectations. It can be easy to get caught up in our instincts, though, and to forget that we need to tackle things logistically. This is where learning how to actively analyze others comes in.

Studies consistently show that we are attracted to confidence and leadership. We like to take the burdens of everyday life and put them on other people's shoulders. Part of this is allowing ourselves to be far too trusting in situations where we would benefit from awareness surrounding red flags. Unfortunately, people are not always genuine; they can be terrible–evil, even. This is a world where we need to be on high alert. While analyzing people will help you in many aspects, such as work and in leadership roles, it can also help keep you safe.

Being situationally aware is simply not in practice anymore. People are constantly unaware of their surroundings and putting themselves in harm's way as a result.

So, as you can see, there are many reasons to unravel

the techniques of analyzation. Scanning people for warning signs or just for information about them puts you ahead of the pack. There is nothing more beneficial to your life, your relationships, and your protection. Spot narcissists before they have a chance to victimize you. Understand your boss's motives and learn how to nail down what they want from you, without even hearing them say it.

Here are some jobs which actively employ analyzing others:

- Politicians

- Lawyers

- Criminal investigators

- Military officials

- Psych professionals

- Forensic experts

As you can see, it truly is a universal tool. Many different people have to analyze others daily in their day-to-day lives.

I hope that these are the skills you want to learn. They

are invaluable, and it is my pleasure to help you improve your life, one impression at a time.

There are, of course, incredible benefits to consuming the knowledge I am offering to you today. First off, you will find that you can communicate your needs to other people far more effectively. Being able to tell how they are reacting and changing your approach accordingly is more than helpful. Communication is the most important skill that we can hone, quite frankly. It helps ease tension, earn the confidence of others, and put us in a positive light. Emotional intelligence goes hand in hand with communication as well.

This is another skill that will be furthered when paired with the power to analyze others. Your emotional intelligence greatly relies on your ability to understand others. The goal is always to meet people where they are: understanding what they need and being able to tell how they need to be handled. Whether you lead a team, need to help your children through their struggles, or are feeling the tension in your love life, I am here to help.

Strong relationships are the glue of society and, more importantly, of families. We need to know how to handle our spouses, children, and anybody else directly related to us. Strained relationships lead to strained relations, and none of us want to be caught up in a family feud. Learning how people tick and how to handle tough situations is the key. You will also learn how to watch for red flags with your children. Knowing how to read their body language and pick up on their verbal cues do wonders for seeing warning signs well in advance.

If you are a parent, this will be a key book in taking your parenting to the following level.

As for another skill, leadership, you will soon be at the front of the crowd. You will find that people not only listen to you but that they actively want to listen to you. Becoming a strong leader means being able to tell who a person is just by carefully observing them. True leaders understand the absolute power that body language holds. After all, it is the oldest form of communication of them all.

Many leaders in the business world, as well as in other areas, actively take lessons and classes on analyzing others. This is a skill which can be applied in almost every situation you can think of. It builds your confidence knowing that when you take the lead, others follow suit.

I am pretty sure you are beginning to get the idea of

what analyzing others can do for you. The benefits are boundless, and there are new ones at every corner. You cannot imagine how much life will change!

I would like to get you started with a few rules. As you can imagine, there is a baseline to start when it comes to analyzing others. You can remember some steps to help you begin which are not hard and fast but excellent for helping you to understand the process. Practice makes perfect, so make sure you pay close attention to this list.

These rules are as follows:

1.   Understand What Their Baseline Is: Everybody is just a tad bit different from the rest. It is almost like how parents can tell their twins apart, but nobody else can. Learning how to analyze others means you can tell them apart on a much different level. Understand that you can only tell their "baseline" after knowing them for a while.

You can watch for signs that they are nervous. Perhaps ask probing questions you know will elicit the emotion you want to pin down. If they tend to become physical restless under duress, you know what sort of body language to watch for.

This is the first rule for many reasons. Most importantly, it reminds us that we need to see the whole person. Cold reading is great.

2.	Notice the Changes: Take into account the entire picture of the person. This builds off of the first rule. Understand that any gesture can mean something, but you need to put several clues together to really solve the mystery that is a person.

This will also build off of noticing what signs of nervousness you may be looking for. We are using nervousness for these examples, but it goes for any emotion. Anger, unease, discomfort–they are all negative emotions you can begin to pinpoint.

3.	Watch For Warning Signs. When certain behaviors are brought into the light and therefore meaning in your eyes, you can start to piece it together. If you have noticed that they shift their eyes around when nervous, and their eyes tighten up when they are angry, you will know when you are treading on dangerous territory.

There are several different clusters of behaviors that can be seen across the board. As mentioned, humans are pack animals in nature. This means that we have learned how to communicate with each other whether we like it or not. Certain tip-offs are pretty well-known. However, a lot more will be missed to the untrained eye. That is why you are reading this!

4.   Compare Behavior Changes: The following rule in this line-up is to always make sure you watch how they behave with others as well. It is a popular belief that you do not watch the person who is speaking–you watch the reaction of the person you want to impress. Making sure you are taking note of your boss's body language while listening to co-workers, for example.

Notice the changes between them talking to you and them talking to others. This will help cue you into their true emotions about you as well as how they feel about others. Are their arms crossing when they talk to their friends? Is their body still turned towards you even while engaged in conversation elsewhere?

5.   Watch Yourself. One of the most powerful things you can do is be aware of your body language. We do not just need to understand others but also ourselves. We influence others with our facial expressions without even knowing what it looks like. That

is not what you want to be doing. To control a situation or a conversation, or even influence it, you need to practice expressions.

The best way to do this is to do it in the mirror.

6. Listen To Others Talk. Identify the strongest person in the room. You will notice them right away, most likely. Sometimes, however, it takes a little time. Look for open body language being used purposefully but elegantly. A big smile, a voice that commands attention and self-confidence are all ways of saying "I am the boss in this situation." They do not need the approval of others and they often hold the most sway in the situation.

Same idea as watching the boss when others are talking. Even if somebody is technically the boss, that does not mean they are completely in control. A confident, strong person will make an impression and quickly become somebody whose opinion the "head honcho" deeply trusts. Knowing which strings to pull will push you further and further toward getting what you want out of a situation.

7. Watch Them Move. Looking at body language while they talk to you, especially sitting or

standing still, is one thing. You also need to watch their general state of being while moving around. You can tell quite a bit about a person just by the way they walk and how they move. Confident people tend to stand tall, with their shoulders back and chest pushed a little out. They walk with purpose, as though they always have somewhere important to be.

On the other hand, somebody who is unsure of themselves embodies the exact opposite traits. They try to make themselves look small, perhaps hunching over a little, keeping their head low.

8.   Listen For Speech Patterns. Another rule is to listen closely to how they talk and what they are saying, both about the topic at hand and about themselves. How a person speaks tells you so much about them, both literally and figuratively! When you can identify how they speak when they are being truthful and genuine, you can figure out when they are being the opposite.

There are several different ways to go about this. However, looking for "action words" is one of the best. A lot of ex-agents talk about how looking for these words, especially strong verbs; it helps you figure out how their brain works. These words do not just convey their thoughts but they convey the patterns of their thoughts as well.

9.   Key Into Their Personality. The last rule is to always put all of this information together. You cannot use one of these rules without following up with the others. These are the cardinal tenets off of which all analyzation of others is built. Once you put together their verbal communication, their body language, and understand them as a whole, you have won half the battle.

It is especially important in the art of analyzing people that you follow this rule. Humans are, by nature, endlessly complex. We cannot be understood by just one piece of information or even a few pieces. Think of it like putting together a puzzle. In the beginning, you have no idea what the result will be. Once you begin to put some of the pieces together, you begin to understand the whole picture. You can even fill in some of the missing pictures once you have enough of those pieces.

So, as you can see, you eventually will build your skillset until you can fill in more information with only some of the pieces. But you still need those pieces.

These rules should be followed at all times. Keep them in mind whenever you go about trying to figure anybody out. They are key in your journey through the art of analyzation!

It can be easy to misunderstand which is which, especially when dealing with potentially dangerous situations. However, mixing them up due to inexperience or simply not knowing the difference can be far more troublesome. Paranoia at its most extreme form is a symptom of many mental illnesses. None of us are immune to falling into the trap of poor thought patterns which encourage paranoia to take hold. It is a sinister feeling that we all need to keep at bay.

Intuition is rooted almost solely in logic. It is the idea that you have cultivated an array of experiences in your life that you can compare to the situation at hand. It is a result of insight as well as the ability to properly analyze others. You will feel calm, stable, and rational when your intuition is kicking in. It does not feel like it is "forced" upon you in the same way that fear does. You have control over intuition and can reason your way through even the negative thoughts that come your way.

You can ascribe the following words to intuition:

- Collected

- In control

- Gentle

- Freeing

- Enlightening

As you can see, intuition is a highly positive emotion you should nurture. Always listen to that inner voice which nudges you towards good ideas. With a little bit of attention, you can quickly decide whether it is intuition you are feeling or simply anxiety and fear.

Speaking of which, let us talk a little bit about fear now. This is a strong emotion that overwhelms you. Fear eats away and pushes you towards rash behavior. You know fear well—we all do. This is an emotion we have all felt, probably many times over our lifespans. You cannot count how many times it has crept into your brain. It is not just an emotion, however.

It is something far more powerful. Fear can actively change the way you think and your ability to respond to situations. The part of the brain which controls it, the amygdala, shows signs of hyperactivity when you feel fear, and your frontal lobe's activity is stunted. These two regions are responsible for your reactions, your impulses, and your behavior.

Those are not the parts of yourself that you want to fall short on!

If it is fear you are feeling, the following words may suit it:

- Apprehensive

- Impulsive

- Irrational

- Cagey

- Insecure

Once you begin to tell the difference, you begin to take control back. Managing your negative emotions properly is one of the best steps in building your self-control. It also allows you to stay focused on situations even if they feel dangerous in any way.

Techniques Of Dark Psychology And Dark Manipulation

When it comes to the idea of influencing people, there are several techniques in dark psychology that are often used for this purpose. Typically, people use techniques of mind control to influence others. These techniques have been known to humans for several years.

Most people are fascinated by the thought of the possibility of someone being able to control their minds. Basically, this fascination is laced by fears of the possibilities of another person influencing them by being able to control their minds and get them to do things against their will.

There are a lot of conspiracy theories about the way governments and those in positions of power influence people by controlling their minds and getting them to do things against their will. As a matter of fact, there have been court cases where defendants claim that they committed the crimes they are being accused of as a result of the influence of brainwashing.

Regardless of the fact that many people talk about the influence of mind control, very little is yet known by most people about the different techniques of dark psychology that can be used to influence people through mind control, and the mode of operation of each of these techniques.

Though there are many ways of influencing people, the techniques of mind control are the most common, and they are brainwashing, persuasion, hypnosis, manipulation, and deception.

Brainwashing

Brainwashing is simply a way of convincing people to let go of those things that they hitherto believed in so that they can pick up new values and ethics. There are several ways in which this type of influence is exerted, though not all of them fall under dark psychology.

Take a person who has traveled to live in a different country, for example. Chances are the person who is going to be influenced by certain factors of change as a result of his new environment so that the person can easily fit into and function in his new society.

Dark psychology, on the other hand, is manifested when a dictator takes over power and tries to brainwash his/her subjects to accept his dictates in order to rule peacefully. This type of influence also manifests in concentration camps.

There are, however, a lot of misconceptions about the topic of brainwashing. When it comes to exerting this kind of influence, some people have some perverted ideas about the practice, and this includes techniques used by governments to influence their subjects, which they seem to manipulate like a remote control.

Also, there are people who do not seem to believe in the efficacy of brainwashing, so they think people are lying when they claim to have been brainwashed.

When people are being brainwashed, they will be convinced to change their viewpoint on a particular subject by making use of different strategies to influence the way they think and see things. During this process, people do not merely rely on a single strategy, and for this reason, one cannot easily capture the practice into a single idea or thought.

Typically, the targets of brainwashing get isolated from the things they are familiar with, and their emotions will become broken such that they become vulnerable. It is in this state of emotional vulnerability that new concepts are introduced to them. As the subjects assimilate this concept, the brainwasher rewards them for putting the thoughts into practice or for expressing the thoughts in line with the new ideas.

The reward for putting the new ideas into practice is used for reinforcement for the brainwashing that is taking its course.

Persuasion

This is another technique used in influencing people, and it is closely related to manipulation. The aim of this technique is to influence the character, intentions, attitudes, and beliefs or values of the target. This technique is used everyday dealings with people and institutions.

Sometimes, this influencing technique is an important aspect of communication, which helps to get people of different mindsets to consolidate and agree on a particular subject matter. This technique is used in business to get people to change their mindset about a product, idea, or event that is taking place. To do this, written or spoken words are used to pass thoughts, ideas, feelings, or messages to others.

Persuasion is also used for selfish reasons in order to achieve personal goals. It is commonly used during trials, by sales representatives to give sales pitches and by politicians during electioneering campaigns. Though these reasons may not be considered as bad or evil reasons, they remain dark psychology techniques that are used to get the subject to act or think in a way that is contrary to their original line of thought or reasoning.

Some scholars define persuasion as a technique that makes use of an individual's powers or resources to alter the behavior or attitudes of other people. It is important to note that there are different types of persuasion which are as follows:

Systemic Persuasion: This involves the process of making use of logic and appeals to change and influence other people's ways of life or reasoning.

Heuristic Persuasion: This is the type of persuasion that involves changing a person's attitudes and beliefs by appealing to the person's emotions or habits.

Persuasion, as an agent of dark influence, is always used in every society. Take, for instance, when you are talking to a person about some political or religious ideologies, you are going to try to persuade them to start thinking the way you think. Also, during political campaigns, every politician tries to persuade their listeners to vote for them. A sales representative who is trying to sell a new product to a client tries everything within his/her power to influence the client's decision by trying to persuade him to buy the product he is selling.

Persuasion as a form of influence is so common that people do not even realize that they are being influenced by it at all. The only time it becomes a problem is in cases when a person devotes all of his time to persuade a person to adopt ideals or sets of beliefs that are not in line with his/her own values.

Manipulation

Manipulation is another dark technique that is used in influencing people. There are many ways of using this technique to influence the thought pattern of the target.

To achieve their aim, manipulators use insults, deceits, and other underhanded strategies, and they do their bidding without considering the welfare or the emotions of their targets.

This is a very potent method of dark psychology as it makes use of cunning, abusive, and exploitative methods. Most times, people are able to realize that they are being manipulated, and people are also able to point out the fact that someone close to them is being manipulated, but they do not always regard it as a technique of dark psychology.

Deception

This is also a way of influencing people using dark psychology as a way of controlling the minds of others. Here, the subjects are made to sell ideas, events, or things which are not true or which never happened. These ideas that the agent tries to sell absolute lies or twisted versions of the truth.

Deception also has to do with other things like propaganda, dissimulation, secrecy, disguise, and distraction. This is also a dangerous dark technique as the subject does not also know that dark psychology. They may not easily find out because they have been presented with a lie and made to believe that it's the truth. It gets more difficult when the truth that is being hidden from the subject is something that could keep them away from harm's way.

Manipulation Techniques

As you may already know, manipulators make use of

everything within his power to work so hard to reach his goals and satisfy his selfish needs. To reach these goals, a person who wishes to manipulate another makes use of several techniques to influence people to do the things they want them to do. Five of the most common techniques that are used by manipulators are blackmail, emotional blackmail, debasing others, telling lies, and creating illusions.

Blackmail

This is usually a manipulator's first strategy in trying to influence a target. It is said to be actions that involve threatening someone else. These threats are often not justified, but they are aimed at getting something out of the target or cause them to lose something if they do not do the bidding of the manipulator.

Blackmail can also be said to be a way of coercing someone else by threating them. The agents, in this case, tell the target that they are going to face criminal prosecution and threaten them that they are going to take their money. They may even be threatened with physical harm.

Emotional Blackmail

This is also another strategy that is used by manipulators

to get their subjects to do their bidding. In using this technique, the manipulator induces a feeling of guilt or sympathy in their targets. These emotions are very strong feelings that humans experience, and they are capable of making people act according to the will of the manipulator.

Once these feelings have been induced in the subject, the manipulator takes advantage of the feeling to get what they really want from the subject. With this, it is easy for them to coerce the target to do what they want or help them in a way that they ordinarily wouldn't.

Debasing Others

In order to get others to help them to achieve their goals, another technique that manipulators use is to debase others in order to get them to help them to achieve their goals. This is a technique that has proven to be very easy as the manipulator simply tries to lower the self-esteem of his/her target.

In most cases, the manipulator does not try to verbally debase his subjects because they are going to feel like the manipulator is trying to attach his person, and this will make them raise their guard. In this case, the target will no longer be willing to help the manipulator achieve his or her goals. Hence they begin to keep as much distance as they can from the manipulator, and this will make it hard for them to reach their final goals.

Lying

Regardless of what the aim of the manipulator is, one thing they are always very good at is telling lies, and they are always going to do this till they are able to achieve their goals fully. In order to reach their ultimate goal, there are several types of lies that manipulators tell. They either tell complete lies or leave out some parts of the truth about certain topics.

One of the main reasons why manipulators tell lies is because they are well aware of the fact that the truth is not going to help them to achieve their goals as much as their lies would. Most times, they feel like people may not want to help them if they tell the truth. This means that the truth is going to

ruin their chances of succeeding in what they want completely.

Creating Illusions

This is a technique that the manipulator combines with lying in order to excellently achieve their final goals, regardless of whose ox is gored. They create illusions by creating an image of their choice and then make their target feel like this image, which is an illusion is the reality. It does not matter to the manipulator that the image he has created is not real.

In order to achieve their aims, manipulators go as far as creating shreds of evidence that they need to drive their point home to the point they are trying to prove, in line with their selfish goals.

In creating their illusion, manipulators create ideas in their targets' minds and back the ideas up with evidence. Once they have been able to create these ideas, the manipulators withdraw for some days and watch the effect of their manipulation take its full course in the minds of their targets for some time.

Controlling Others with Confusion and Compulsion

Typically, in dealing with humans, there is always a level of conscious manipulation, coercion, and influence that takes place, but when a relationship is healthy, those involved will be able to strike a balance with time and consistency.

In cases where a person is dealing with another person who has high tendencies of manipulating others, the manipulator has all the power, and he wields this power by confusing and using compulsion on the other person, and they sometimes make the victim feel like they are the ones that are actually in charge.

When a person who is prone to manipulation gets into a relationship with a person who is very manipulative, it is often very dangerous because the manipulator is going to use compulsion on the subject a lot, and he/she is also going to get confused a lot.

Below are some of the ways which manipulators use compulsion and confusion on their targets:

The Manipulator Opens A Trap

Using control and compulsion on a target is not quite different from any other type of manipulation technique. This is much easier when a target is a person that acts in a particular way that they want to harness, and they simply create some positive strokes as often as possible.

Once these strokes are created, one may not see any visible difference as all the parties involved in the relationship are largely at peace with each other at this stage. Everything is normal, and they don't have any issues doing things for the sake of one another. In rare cases, the contrary may be the case, but it only means that things may have started off badly.

The Manipulator Places Bait in The Trap

When the manipulator has successfully confused the target, he then proceeds to place bait on the trap he has set. This may be a direct trap or a camouflaged trap that comes in the form of an offer of a very juicy reward. In work environments, the target may be promised a promotion or a pay rise. In an intimate relationship, the bait may be a sex offer or a promise of a blissful life together forever in marriage.

There are men and women who have become accustomed to the fluctuating nature of their partners who may want them today and not want them tomorrow. Some women have been roped in with the promise of marriage as bait, but never get proposed to even after several years. The reverse may also be the case.

Creating Compulsive Behavior

By setting a trap and placing a bait on the trap, the manipulator is able to cage the subject into their strings, and because the effects of the manipulation is getting the best of them, as well as the stress and uncertainty that comes with it, the victim is usually unable to withdraw a bit to see a clear picture of the things that are really happening and the effects they are having on them.

People that are seeing things from outside, who are not involved in the manipulative relationship are able to notice the way the subject acts whenever they are around the manipulator as opposed to the way they act when they are in the presence of other people, though there is never a clear indicator for the difference in attitude.

In some cases, the manipulator is also able to alter their behavior such that they decide how their subjects act in the presence of other people. This way, their relationship looks healthy before others. Though the victim may seem happier when they are with others, they may not be able to figure out why it is so.

Often times, the manipulators are able to figure out the emotions of their subjects without much struggle. When they seem to be happy for too long, they find ways to bring it down by dampening their spirit.

At this stage, the victim is already used to the intermittent threats and rewards, and he becomes conditioned to act accordingly. These threats or rewards do not necessarily need to have any connection with the behavior of the victim, and this type of treatment creates a compulsive behavior in the victim.

Whenever rewards are linked to the actions of a person, the person's actions stop whenever the rewards are no longer available. When on the other hand, the rewards of action change slowly and inconsistently, people find themselves going on for a long time after they have received the first reward, with hopes of receiving another.

How To Talk

THE POWER OF PERSUASION

The power of persuasion means nothing more than using mental abilities to form words and feelings used to convince other people to do things they may or may not want to do. Some people are better able to persuade than other people. And some people are easier to persuade then other people.

The ease of persuading other people is directly tied to their current mental or emotional state. Someone who is lonely or tired is easier to persuade, simply because their defenses are lowered. Someone who is momentarily needy may be easier to persuade than someone who has a strong sense of self-worth. People who are at a low point in their lives are easy prey for others who might try to persuade them to do something they might not usually do.

Think of the publicity surrounding religious cults in the past. Everyone wanted to know how someone could fall prey to the teachings and ideals of the cult. The answer is simple: the victim was seeking something the cult offered. Whether the dangling carrot was food and shelter or love or religious freedom, the cult offers something tangible to the person who feels their life is lacking something important. And the person who joins the cult does not see themselves as a victim, but a participant. Think back further to the flower children of the sixties and seventies. These people lived in communes where everyone had a particular role to play. Some people would grow gardens to feed the members of the commune while others might wash laundry or clean houses. Everyone helped everyone else. The idea behind living in a commune was to leave behind the trappings that 'society' deemed as markers of success, such as fat paychecks and huge houses. These people wanted to live simply and enjoy what love and Mother Nature had to offer.

For every good group that assembles for the good of the people and works to help its members, there are countless groups that are brought together by forces that have no desire other than controlling other people for their own good. These leaders are very charismatic and very dangerous, because a person who is temporarily weak in mind or in the soul may not be able to resist their promises. It is important for everyone to understand how persuasion works in order to be able to resist it when needed.

The first step in persuasion involves the idea of reciprocating. If a person does something nice for someone else, then the receiving person usually feels the need to do something good in return. If someone helps their elderly neighbor carry in groceries from the car, that neighbor might feel obligated to bake homemade cookies for that person. A coworker who helps complete a project is more likely to receive assistance when it is needed. Many people do nice things for others all the time without expecting anything in return. The person who does nice things for people and then mentions some little favor that can be done in return may be someone to watch closely.

Nonprofit organizations use this tactic to gain more contributions to their causes. They will often send some little trinket or gift to prompt people to donate larger sums of money, or even just to donate where they might not have originally. The idea behind this is that the person opening the letter has received a little gift for no reason, so they might feel obligated to give something in return.

The consistency of self is the following step. People who

commit to something, through verbal or written methods, are more likely to follow through on the idea that someone who makes no promises, Even if the original motivation is gone or the original incentive was taken away, people see this promise as being part of their image. They made a promise. This is often why counselors tell people to write their goals down. People are more likely to follow a written list they can refer to daily.

It is easy enough to change someone's image of themselves, especially if that person is needy or mentally weak. During times of war, it is customary to get prisoners to denounce their own country in order to hopefully turn others against that country. This is easy enough to do when starved prisoners are also mentally weak and have few defenses to use to deflect their captors. By constantly repeating statements that denounce the home country the captive begins to believe what they are saying because it must be true because they are saying it.

Another thing to be careful of is what is known as the herd mentality. Humans live in groups. Most of us want to belong to the herd and want to enjoy the safety being in a herd brings. Monkey see, monkey do. People tend to mirror the behavior seen around them. Think of the story of the emperor that runs around with no clothes on. His tailors had him convinced he was wearing fine garments, so he convinced all the people of his kingdom. And because they could not question the king, they had to believe what he was saying. This can also work in seriously negative ways. Think of the mob mentality. This is just another way to follow the herd, but it usually involves illegal or dangerous activities engaged in only because someone else was doing the same thing.

Some people are automatically tempted to follow authority. People in positions of authority can command blind respect to their authority simply by acting a certain way or putting on a uniform. The problem with this is that authority figures or those that look like authority figures, can cause some people to do extraordinary things they would not normally do had a person in a position of authority not been the one asking. And it is not simply held to people in uniform. People who carry themselves a certain way or speak a certain way can give the impression that they are something they are not.

For someone or something to be considered a credible authority, it must be familiar and people must have trust in the person or organization. Someone who knows all there is to know about a subject is considered an expert and is more likely to be trusted than someone who has limited knowledge of the subject. But the information must also make sense to the people hearing it. If there is not some semblance of accuracy and intelligence then the authority figure loses credibility. Even the person who is acknowledged as an expert will lack persuasive abilities if they are seen as not being trustworthy.

People want to be liked. People want to like other people. The problem is when some people use this fact to cause other people to do things they might not ordinarily do. People who are easy to like usually come across as very persuasive. People want to believe them. Con artists are extremely likeable people. The problem is that even likeable people may not have your personal best interests at heart. In fact, they probably only have their own interest in mind. Even someone who is totally legitimate, like a salesperson, is really most interested in their own interests. They may want their customer to be perfectly happy with their purchase so they will recommend that salesperson to their friends, but their ultimate concern is with themselves and their sales goals.

The worst part of the power that goes along with persuasion is that things that are scarce or hard to get are seen as much more valuable. People value diamonds because they are expensive and beautiful. If they were merely pretty stones, they would not be as interesting. Inconsistent rewards are a lot more interesting than consistent rewards. If a cookie falls every time a person rings a bell, then they are less likely to spend a lot of time ringing the bell because they know the cookie reward will always appear. If, however, the cookie only appears sometimes, people will spend much more time ringing the bell just in case this is the time the cookie will fall.

There are ways to improve the power of persuasion. Just like any other trait, it can be made stronger by following a few strategies and by regular practice.

Never hesitate to ask others what they think. Usually, those in a position of authority will not look for advice from other people. This is an opportunity many leaders neglect to take advantage of. Instead of asking others for their opinion and ideas, they miss the chance to make everyone feel like part of the group with an equal role to play. Besides, leaders who are not afraid to ask for input from others might learn something they did not know before.

Always remember to ask for advice, not feedback. People love being asked to give advice. Asking for feedback means that an opinion has already been given and the speaker wants to know what everyone else thinks of their own opinion. In many situations, there will be no responses because no one wants to disagree or be seen as argumentative, particularly with an authority figure. But asking for advice gives people a chance to voice their own opinions.

Before asking for any type of assistance, set the stage. People do not like being put on the spot. Walking up to someone and immediately asking for a favor sends two messages. The first one is that the favor is more important than the person. In this case, the favor needed is the focus of the conversation. Say that Bob walks into the room, goes straight up to Bill and asks Bill to assist at a fundraiser that weekend. Bill is caught off guard and must make an immediate decision. Does he say no, in front of others, and look like a mean-spirited person for not helping at the fundraiser? Or does he answer with yes without really knowing if he wants to do it or not?

Now if Bob had bothered to set the stage for asking for the favor, he would have approached the conversation in a totally different manner. First, he would have approached Bill with a friendly greeting and cheerful smile. He would take a few minutes to make small talk with Bill, perhaps asking about his work life or his family life. After chatting cheerfully for a few minutes Bob would approach the idea of the fundraiser in a casual manner. "Hey, Bill, by the way...." He would explain what he needed Bill to do, explain how much he would really enjoy having Bill's presence at the fundraiser, then asking Bill to get back with him as soon as possible with an answer. He would assure Bill that whatever decision he made would be fine, although he really hoped Bill would be able to join him.

What is the difference between the two situations? In the second situation, Bill feels wanted. He feels needed. He feels as though his presence, or the lack of it, is important to Bob. In the second situation, Bob is most likely to get an honest answer. And what if Bill is not able to help Bob at the fundraiser? Bill will be more likely to help Bob in the future because he not only feels valued but he feels like he owes Bob something, Bill would probably be thinking that he owed Bob one in the future.

Persuasion is a powerful tool in the game of life. Persuasive people know that they have an amazing power, and they know how to use it correctly. They know how to listen and really hear what other people have to say. They are very good at making a connection with other people, and this makes them seem even more honest and friendly. They make others feel that they are knowledgeable and can offer a certain sense of satisfaction. They also know when to momentarily retreat and regroup. They are not pushy. They are persuasive.

Conversational Skills Techniques

When people don't answer you, when they use sarcasm, telling you it's impossible to talk to you, threatening you with ultimatums, or talking to you like you were a child, these signs of psychological manipulation through language and communication are exhausting. This is a form of emotional abuse and mental exploitation that we must learn to recognize.

One of the most sinister men in Italian history was Licio Gelli. He was an agent of the Masonic Lodge Propaganda Due. He was a neo-fascist who specialized in manipulating masses. This evil person once said that to control anyone, you had to know how to communicate. He showed us that language can be used as a weapon and can be used to dominate.

Many people know this too well. Within the realm of politics, in media, in advertising there is constant use of manipulation to control us, influence our decisions, and yes, to seduce us. Once we come into our private realm, everything gets a bit more complex and mantic.

We are talking about the way we communicate with our friends, significant other, family, etc. If you just stop and look, you can see signs of emotional and psychological manipulation all around you, but these are usually camouflaged. You might also fall into a trap of using it yourselves. You must know how to detect it and how to react to it.

You must know that it isn't just important to watch what you say but how you say it.

Signs of Psychological Manipulation

When we talk about psychological manipulation by using words, what happens first will be an imbalance in a relationship. It is using language to benefit yourself. Not to just control a person but to harm them as well. Bare emotions are what cause this aggression in you.

Aldous Huxley once said that words are like X-rays. If they are used in a Machiavellian way, they could pierce through everything: another person's self-esteem, their identity, and dignity. You must learn to see them coming, to know a bit more about this personally. Here are some warning signs:

Manipulating facts

Anyone who is an expert in manipulating through communication is a strategist who is great at twisting the truth. They will always turn everything around to their favor, lower their share of responsibility, and blame anyone but themselves. They will also withhold and exaggerate important information to make sure the balance will always tilt toward their "truth."

They say you are impossible to talk to

This approach is effective, direct, and very simple. If anyone tells you that "you are impossible to talk to," they are avoiding exactly what you are wanting to do: talking about the problem. It's common for them to say you are too emotional, you are "making a mountain out of a molehill," and they can't talk with you. They will accuse you of what they have problems with, and this is poor communication skills.

Harassing intellectually

An emotional and psychological manipulator uses another common strategy: intellectual harassment. They will constantly throw arguments your way. They will also make sure the information is different and the facts are so twisted just trying to emotionally exhaust you and convince you that they are correct.

Ultimatums with no time to decide

You might have heard someone say: "If you can't accept what I am saying, then it's all over." They might have gone one further with you have until tomorrow to think about it. This communication style is very distressing and painful. They have put you between a rock and a hard place and generate a lot of emotional suffering along with anxiety.

You must know that is somebody respects you, and truly loves you, they will never use "all or nothing" threats. This is just one more manipulation strategy.

Constantly saying your name while talking

If somebody constantly says your name during a heated conversation, they are using a control mechanism. When they do this, they are forcing you to pay attention and causing you to feel intimidated.

Black humor and irony

If they like using black humor and irony, they are trying to ridicule and humiliate you. This is another sign of psychological manipulation in communication. They are trying to belittle you and trying to impose their superiority on you.

Using evasiveness or silence

If they say things like: "Now isn't a good time", "I don't want to talk about it", "Why are you bringing that up now?" All of this is common with significant others, especially if one doesn't have a good sense of responsibility or communication skills.

Claiming ignorance

If somebody says to you: "I don't understand what you mean," this is another tactic. They will pretend not to understand what you are wanting them to do or say. They are playing mind games. They want to make it look like you are complicating things and the conversation doesn't make any sense. This is a strategy that passive-aggressive manipulators like to use to avoid taking responsibility and wants to make you suffer.

They allow you to talk first

The most subtle sign of psychological manipulation is when they always make you talk first. By doing this, they achieve many things. The first one is buying time to get their argument ready. The second is to figure out your weak points. It is common that after they have listened to you, they won't express their opinion or ideas. They will only ask more questions. Rather than reaching some sort of an agreement, they try to highlight your shortcomings. They will direct the conversation in ways that make you look weak and clumsy.

Yes, there are many other strategies that emotional and psychological manipulator could use when communicating but the above are the most common. These try to intimidate you and keep you from establishing effective dialogues, but they try to subdue you. They are trying to incapacitate you on all levels: mentally, emotionally, and personally. You must learn how to see these destructive strategies.

Silent Treatment = Emotional Abuse

what does "silent treatment" mean? It is refusing to verbally engage with another person, often because of a conflict within the relationship. Some refer to it as stonewalling or the cold shoulder. It is used as a passive-aggressive way to control others. It can be considered emotional abuse. If you think it is normal for your significant other to go for days without speaking to you, think again. Silence can be used productively like right after a breakup or if you are taking a time to cool off but prolonged times of unresponsiveness in relationships aren't healthy or normal.

At times, you might not have anything to say. Sometimes disconnecting is a good idea so that each party can take a moment to reflect on what has happened and then come back once they have received some clarity. Arguments aren't ever pleasant, but they come and go and might leave new understanding.

Most of us have been at a place where we don't want to face the argument and it is not because we fear an escalation. We refuse to go back in because we are trying to punish them.

The silent treatment is one of the most powerful tools that a passive-aggressive manipulator could use. It keeps their opponent on edge while giving you a sense of power. It demands emotional and mental perfection from other people that don't exist in anyone. Ignoring somebody like this is very hurtful. All the emotional effects might last and frankly, this is very unfair.

Dealing with It

If you are the one that is being ignored and you want to work through it, what can you do about it?

Apologize? Grovel? They are useless because the goal of the silent treatment is to make you suffer. You don't want yourself to suffer. You also don't want your loved one to feel like they must trap you into suffering in order to have control over you.

In order to react to this treatment requires a dose of humility, understanding, openness, and sensitivity. What you can do is simple, and you don't have to "take the high road" in the situation. Stances like this are just variations of you falling right into the trap they set because you will soon get tired of trying to fix things.

What you can do is be honest, since this is what you want from them, right? You can say something like: "I would really love to figure out what is wrong," since it requires two people to have an argument.

You must be sincere, and you shouldn't pretend that you haven't noticed their silent treatment; that is simply putting gas on a fire. Acting honestly won't be easy because you will be confused. You feel hurt and guilty, which is a dangerous mix. Creating this mixture of feelings is what the manipulator wants. They want you to be voiceless and feel horrible, which makes you feel terrible.

When you are faced with the silent treatment, it's like trying to play a game of Clue with the board flipped over and without any pieces. You want to be able to solve the problem, but this has more to do with not knowing what you have done wrong or something so tiny the silencer feels the need to control the relationship for some time.

Being the receiver of this manipulation is extremely hard. Not understanding what was done, not understanding what you should say, your feelings being disrespected and disregarded, all the doubts that are planted on if the relationship was viable, as well as the guilt of feeling you created a crack in something wonderful, is a game you will eventually lose. It doesn't do anything but drop more anger onto a volatile situation.

Getting out of this type of situation will take a lot of patience. This is what is needed if you want to continue the relationship. The silencer's cycle of allowing you to come back is just a blame game that they have thought up for you to overlook any damage that they have caused.

Simplicity

Feeling like you have fed your significant other poison and you are struggling to find a way to fix it is no way to live. Don't accept anyone's ploy for power, never internalize it, and don't accept it as being a sign that you are a failure. Understand this, you didn't do anything wrong. Having a grievance is one thing, but constantly being treated unfairly from others isn't.

If you are emotionally abusive, overbearing, or manipulative, too, there isn't anything you should do but say goodbye to each other. The silent treatment's main purpose is to wear you down. Granted, we have heard all sorts of advice from others about love. Communication and love aren't a game of picking sides, keeping score, or winning.

There are two rules that will serve us well during our time here: "Being good to each other and being good for each other." This type of situation isn't an either, or. This is an "and" situation and you must make sure it stays that way, or you will spin out of control.

Using the silent treatment isn't a good way to satisfy these things. And no matter what anybody else has to say, the single word, Hi, can provide you with satisfaction. This hi may be awkward, and it could make you feel like you are drowning or like a restrained panther, but it must be said.

Reality is a great place to start a conversation. But silence can sometimes sound like a scream

When is Silent Treatment Right?

There is a place and time for silence. There are circumstances where silence is recommended. In toxic relationships where one person tries to resolve the conflict, but the aggression is escalated silence is acceptable. Staying quiet is a way to help you cope with the person and situation. Silence can be used to protect and to help calm down after an altercation.

Silence can also be used as a boundary if you have just removed yourself from a relationship with a sociopath or narcissist.

How to Know if Silence is Abusive

You must ask yourself: "Am I being forced to defend myself or am I the one attacking them?" This is where you will find the difference. If you remain silent just to gain an upper hand and to make them suffer, then that is abuse.

If you keep your mouth shut to avoid suffering abuse, that is self-defense. If you aren't sure, it will help to answer these following few questions:

You are calm again, but you still expect them to make the following move.

When an argument happens, it might take time for feelings to come back down. Silence in these situations isn't bad since it can keep you doing or saying something you might regret.

If you are staying silent, act after you have calmed down since you will insist that they make the first move toward reconciliation. This is a bit abusive. If you want to talk, open a dialogue.

Will just a complete apology do?

Will you stay silent for as long as they don't give you an apology? They might have shown some remorse and are trying to make amends. It isn't what you had in mind while you are ruminating. If efforts have been made toward an apology, it is right for you to move from your position to end the treatment you have given them.

This isn't saying that you have forgiven them, but you should have a conversation about what happened and why it makes you feel like you do. When you don't engage, you are choosing to keep them back which might be emotional abuse.

Are you responsible for the disagreement?

At times the other person is completely wrong. There are things that aren't excusable. This isn't always the case. If you are keeping silent despite fault falling at your feet, you are ignoring the role you had in the argument that led you to where you are. This is abusive because it puts all the blame on the other person and makes them feel bad.

Will you keep this up for a certain time frame?

When somebody does something that annoys you, don't think that you aren't going to talk with them for the remainder of the day. This can be viewed as abusive since it is giving a sentence for the crime, no matter how you may feel at any time in the future. It is telling the other person they deserve this punishment. It doesn't leave any room for forgiveness or feelings getting better between the two of you.

Secrets of Persuasive People, How to Stop And Spot Manipulation

Manipulation is about control and gain. They need to control a person and the situation in order to get whatever it is they are after. While each set of circumstances are different, there are still some very common tactics that manipulators use, think of them as a general blueprint. They can be altered a bit based on certain situations, but they are all generally the same. The ways in which people can be manipulated are also different; for instance, the way someone manipulates someone in a romantic relationship is not going to be same in friendship and so on. The good news is that the basic principles are similar enough that if you learn to spot one manipulative situation, it can make it easier to spot more in the future.

No matter what type of situation, manipulators still have similar tactics that they will use simply because they work. They will change them a bit depending on their specific wants and the situation at hand, but manipulative behavior is not the norm so it can still be spotted if you know what you're looking for. Even if they think they are breaking the mold, a manipulator is doing what countless manipulators have done before them. This doesn't make their behavior any better or acceptable, but it does make them somewhat predictable. If you are the victim of manipulation, you might be able to see it for what it is, but others do, and this is important because when you want to cut a manipulator out of your life, those are the people you can depend on.

Common Forms of Manipulation

• One of the most used forms of manipulation is someone making you think they are better or above you. They might treat you as if you are a child or throw condescending looks or tones your way when you interact with them. Sometimes it can even go as far as to simply tell you that that they know better and their way is the best and only way. However, it happens, the message is clear, they're the 'superior,' and you are the 'inferior.' This is emotionally exhausting and beats down a person's self-esteem making it less likely that the manipulator will be challenged because at a point, you just stop speaking up because it never worked, to begin with.

• Making jokes at your expense is another common tactic used by manipulators. This is especially awful because it is not done in private. It is used as a method of putting someone down and making them feel small, and in order to do this, they need a group of people laughing. Sadly, this method has only grown in popularity because of the use of social media, where it is abundant. The jokes can range from physical attributes to how a person dresses, but either way, you are meant to be the butt of the joke and laughed at. When the manipulator is confronted, they usually come back with things like, "I was only kidding, you're too sensitive," making it seem like you are the problem.

• Sometimes all it takes is a look to manipulate someone. This might seem childish, but a facial expression has just as much power as words. Manipulators master the art of the death glare, the condescending head tilt, eye rolling, and shaking their head. Any facial expression or gesture that indicates to you, without words to back down. Even though this seems like something that you wouldn't fall victim to, it can and does happen. As a matter of fact, this type of manipulation can mean stop, you're wrong, you're ridiculous, and many other things that lower your self-esteem. And to make it worse, all of it with no words spoken.

• Another common tactic is to simply ignore someone, for instance saying hello to everyone in the room except you; this can be demeaning and hurtful, not to mention also just embarrassing. Part of this is also acting bored, disinterested, and inconvenienced even when you are simply talking about everyday things. Going right along with this, they will often not answer any questions, phone calls, emails, text messages, and always seems unavailable. Many manipulators do this because they know it makes someone feel inferior, and they hope the person will go out of their way to understand what they did wrong and make up for it when in reality they did nothing wrong, and the manipulator is just using them for control and to gain something from the situation.

• Guilt tripping is another common way for manipulators to get what they want, this comes out in the language they use which typically involves things such as, "I thought we were friends, I thought I could count on you, I can't believe how selfish you're being," and so on. This is a powerful way to exert control over the other person because they will wonder if what are saying is true and they will want to do everything in their power to fix it since they thought they were friends, and they will want to fix the friendship. That is when the demands come in from the manipulator, thus giving them what they wanted, at the expense of the other person's feelings.

• Some manipulative people choose to be deliberately difficult, making others cater to their whim in order to make them feel better. The more giving and agreeable you are to them, the more difficult they will be escalating the situation and blowing it out of proportion so they can have more control of the situation and wait until the other person goes out of their way to fix the situation.

• Overly complimenting people and telling them what they want to hear is also a great way for manipulators to get what they want, they are often called sweet talkers, and they mean nothing they say. They know people like to be complimented, and they use this to their advantage. They will tell you what you want to hear. However, it does not end there. They do this because they know it is one of the best ways to make friends, build trust, and then lower the other person's defenses, which is when the true manipulation can begin. They make it seem like all the praise they have been giving is worthy of something in return, and that is when they name their price. This tactic is also even more deplorable because the closer you are to someone, the easier it is for someone to manipulate you because there has been a friendship or relationship that involves trust that has already been cultivated.

The basic rules remain the same, but with different elements added to it to match the different types of circumstances. Even if they think they are masterminds and you are beneath them, the truth is, a manipulative person is not. They have just learned to use their behavior to get what they want to the point of not caring about others. They are not invisible; you can see them for what they are when you know what to look for.

There are also ways to determine whether or not you are in a manipulative friendship as well. Since manipulators use different relationships as a way to manipulate others, friendships are definitely not safe from these people either.

Manipulative Friends

• Not listening: Friends should listen what each other has to say, if you have a friend that expects you to listen to them, but does not return the favor, the chances are that friend has negative intentions. You might get the feeling that your friend is listening because they are looking at you, but instead of sincerity behind the action, it feels more like they are looking right through you. They are not retaining any of the information and are just going through the actions because they think they need to, in order to keep you in their lives. Everyone has bad days, so if this happens once, chances are your friend is just having a bad day, but it this continues to happen, then that is the red flag you were looking for.

• The gossiper: If you have a friend that never has anything nice to say, especially about the rest of the friend group, this too is a sign of manipulation. Manipulators like to stir the pot and will do nearly anything to do so. One of the ways they do this in a friend group is by keeping everyone on their toes by constantly spreading gossip and secrets.

• Out of touch: You might have that friend that only reaches out to you when they need something and seem to be missing in action when you do. This is not a healthy friendship because it sends the message that they only have time for you on their terms and your life doesn't really matter. This can cause self-doubt and low self-esteem. If you feel like you are constantly doing favors for this person and they never help you in return, this is not a true friendship.

• Guilt: Using guilt within a friendship is different than most other relationships because there are other people involved. In cases of guilt, the manipulative person might claim that you have to help them after everything you've done for them. Another hallmark of a manipulative friend and guilt is rallying other people or at least making you think so. They might say things like "even so and so says I'm right and you're wrong." This serves as a way to isolate you, making you more likely to apologize and join their side, for whatever it is they are after.

• Bossy: There is a difference from having a friend leader, the one who is just naturally good at organizing things and planning, and someone is intentionally bossy regardless of how the rest of the group feels. One of the best ways to understand out which is which, if someone gets mad at you if you don't like their idea, that is not a leader that is someone who is trying to be in control constantly, and that is classic manipulative behavior. They will ignore any reasonable suggestions that contradict what they want and will do anything they can to convince you to be on their side.

•   So many favors: This can be tricky because friends do favors for one another and that is completely healthy and normal, it's good to have people to count on. However, if you have a friend that is constantly asking for favors and never seems to have the time to reciprocate, this is unhealthy. They will ask you to do things regardless of what is happening in your life, taking your time away from things that are important to you. This contributes to the feeling of a loss of self.

I

if you think that you have a manipulative friend, it can be difficult because other people are involved. So, one of the best things you can do, so as not to cause too much drama and split up a friend group, which could happen, is to distance yourself from that one person. You can do this by not doing the favors they ask you to do, or not asking them to do anything for you. Create plans and let everyone else know the game plan; this gives the manipulator less opportunity to want to change plans because everyone else will already be on board.

Having a manipulative person in a friend group is difficult because it puts you in a tough spot if you are the only one who notices and knows what they're doing. The good news is, they are your friends too, and at some point, if the manipulative person begins acting in a way that puts too much strain on your friendships, it might be time to sit your friends down and tell them what you know. The best way to go about doing this, should it come to it, is to approach them as a group and calmly explain what manipulation is and how it works. Then use examples of how the friend in question has been treating not only you, but how you have seen them treat your other friends too.

Then, you will want to let them share their own personal experiences with the person as well, because sometimes saying it out loud will help understand how they have manipulated and hurt. Do not force them into saying anything; sometimes people are ashamed of how they have acted out of the ordinary because of the influence of someone else. That is why sharing your story first helps others to feel more comfortable talking about what has happened to them. Once everyone has talked about how they have been manipulated by that person, it is time for you and the rest of the group to decide what to do. Explain to them that confronting the person might just cause more issues and that if they have been manipulating everyone the whole time without caring about their feelings, that is probably not going to change.

More often than not, people are going to want to give someone another chance, and if that is what is decided, reiterate what manipulation is and how to tell when you are being manipulated. Encourage them to tell one another if the person engages in this type of behavior again. It is a good idea to make it clear that if they do, then the best thing for everyone is to stop being friends with them because even if the person apologizes, but makes no effort to change their behavior, nothing will change. It is for the best of everyone that the manipulator not be included anymore because that is what is healthiest.

Be A Positive Influence On Others

No matter which type of manipulation we talk about, Tricks and techniques are necessary to apply them in real life. It's true that those tricks which is used for negative manipulation are mostly decisive. But in the case of persuasion, the techniques can lead to a positive conclusion and to something great.

Now the question is how can manipulation be ethical or how can we differentiate between negative manipulation and persuasion. What are the steps or techniques?

What makes Persuasion Ethical?

Here's the facts about how can manipulation be ethical. First of all, most of us address these criteria as if it is a negative thing just because of the use of manipulation. The reality is, every single existence has two aspects, one is bright and another is dark side. The value of everything depends on our way of acting upon them, manipulation can be used for both good and evil purpose. The user is on the driving seat, so if it is driven through the dark path, not the method of manipulation but the user of it is to blame. It is our goal to manipulate anyone only to bring good results. If we want, we can apply a series of negative manipulation with a goal to deceive someone and make them do what we want. Or we can concentrate on the betterment of others. On that note, the right choice differentiates between the positive and negative sides. This is what makes manipulation a critical thing to practice.

Why Positive Manipulation methods are used

Positive manipulation or persuasion method can be so much helpful for the self-development of any individual. There are so many self-development skills based on which, a person can improve his/her life. There also are many situations where manipulation methods are being used. All those reasons and facts are described below.

Influence: Ethical manipulation is basically fully depended on influence. Influencing other individuals according to their need or influencing someone you know to do something for the betterment of that person, influencing to change habits, behavior all these are beneficial for the society and to improve social communication. In our daily life none can pass a single day without any influence. With or without our knowledge, we are being influenced by others and various desirable things in every aspect and almost always. Being influenced by good things are always appreciated. For example, if an addict quits being influenced by a good person, or you become influenced by the idea of buying a new iPhone-XI can drive you to earn more money. You can see both ideas are beneficial.

Persuasion: There are many times in our life when we face difficulties to make certain decisions or to deal with someone. Suppose it is your co-worker who does not agree with whatever you said, or any decision you have made. What are you supposed to do? The answer is you need to persuade that person by reasoning, or by making him see the benefits of doing what you decided. As long as the argument you are having remains honest, it falls within the criteria of persuasion.

Inspiration: Inspiration is something which is so much helpful if someone wants to manipulate anyone. Suppose someone is playing video games. If he/she keeps winning in the game, he/she gets inspired to play more. Or in the case of a depressed individual, he/she she needs inspiration and motivation in order to get back at the race of life. Inspiring someone to do something either good or bad is basic manipulation tactic.

Unity: Humans have a need of manipulation with almost everyone in their life. It can be someone they just met or someone they have known for a long time, like family members or friends. In the case of a stranger you just need to be logical but to manipulate someone you have known for a long time, unity is necessary. Suppose you want to propose a trip to Las Vegas upcoming summer. Now if your friends do not trust you, they most probably would not want to go. On the other hand, if you had built unity among your circle, they would trust you more, therefore agree to join you. Same goes for family relations. Unity is built upon trust. If someone does not trust you, he/she will not listen to you. How can you manipulate someone who will not listen to you?

For Self Defense: There are so many advantages of learning about the ethical manipulation. This can not only help you carry out your duties but also it can help you to defend yourself. There could be some situation where you need to defend yourself. Suppose someone alleged you about a certain matter as a negative view. Or maybe someone wants to pick a fight with you just because he/she feels like it. What can you do about it? Now if you know manipulation tricks, you can reason with him/her, if that does not work, you can make others around you to judge the situation and have them support you. So, if you know about ethical manipulation, you can easily defend yourself without any worries.

Reasons behind Compliance Manipulation's Ineffectiveness

At this part of the book, we are going to discuss some of the ethical manipulation techniques which can be used in every kind of situation. But in order to use these techniques, we must need to have the full understanding of the topic persuasion. This is usually important to become aware of, since persuasion can easily get confused with pressuring others into conformity. The second option is often focused only on changing the actions of other people by force or blackmailing, while persuasion techniques try to receive persons or groups to look and believe confidently about the thoughts or activities you would like for them to possess.

Manipulation for Compliance: There are lots of ways to manipulate people into complying with your ideas. Some illustrations of this are certainly not threats of legal action if you don't follow laws and regulations, neither is parents intimidating their child with punishment for not doing what they were told. These are not exampling of people complying, rather forcefully making others do something. Making a deal is a good example of people complying. Someone agreeing to do something for in exchange for something is the elaborated version of what I just said. Imagine your child refusing to complete his home task, you know he loves chocolate. Now if you offer to buy him chocolate only if he does his homework, there is a very good chance that he would listen to you now. Because he wants chocolate, and he knows to get chocolate he needs to complete his homework. Therefore, he complies. This can be applied on a much larger and much serious scale too.

Resentment and a Lack of Motivation: The problem with the type of techniques listed above is that without the greed or any benefit, individuals would not agree with or follow you. In addition to this, none relishes being negatively changed, signifying that they happen to become substantially even more extreme. They are most likely to search your replacement, once they discover what their normal spending criteria is. Lamentably, this sort of tricks nowadays is normally rampant, but although at some instances, it's absolutely is an amazingly top-notch or strong program.

When you look back again at being manipulated into compliance, perhaps simply by authorities at institution, bosses at work, or your own parents when you were young, you would feel as if you were used. It generally is not a very good feeling. In addition to that, it often causes negative emotions and interactions, and this is normally because it is structured on dread, rather than free of charge will and decision. How is it normally imaginable to get people to hold out what you would like them to hold out of their exceptional volition? They must make the decision themselves if they happen to plan to continue choosing it.

Using NLP and Creating Agreement for Successful Positive Manipulation

As we know from the discussions earlier, NLP and manipulation are inter related and those techniques can be applied on every kinds of people in order to gain succession. In the process of ethical or positive manipulation, it is not that much easy to apply manipulation and NLP on all the people.

Here are some factors and elements of NLP which can be used for successful positive manipulation.

Connect: Persuasion comes up with a view to connect

with the individuals as this is one of the most important way of knowing other people. As we all know there are so many factors regarding ethical manipulation. The practice of connecting with others makes the process of persuasion pretty much easier. It also helps to blend in with all the people who are around the individual you are trying to persuade. In the regular life of any person, there are so many people they might need to stay with, they might need to blend in with. This certain skill called connecting is unavoidable for all of them.

Trust: Trust is something which is not that much easy for anyone to gain but so much easier to lose. None can ever try to persuade anyone without this certain quality. To be exact, whenever anyone tries to get close to anyone, they must be trustworthy. This certain quality gives us the power to do whatever we want to do, whenever we want to do. Here is an example of the importance of trust. Suppose you want to get close to a certain person for the betterment of that person or because you care about the person. That person isn't going to listen to your words, unless that person has the faith /trust upon you. This is one of those Neuro-Linguistic methods which is a must for the ethical manipulation.

Breaking Patterns: In addition to building any

relationship, additional NLP methods exist for strong subliminal influence. One case in point of this is usually utilizing issues to re-direct someone's concentration or focus to something else, or to snooze mental habits. Issues which need to be ignored because they are hard to provide answers to. Our intellects quickly prefer to make an effort to fix issues even before they are asked.

Storytelling and Metaphors: By the term storytelling and metaphors, we understand very little. It may be hard to understand what we are trying to indicate. Here are the details for those term, when you are in the middle of the persuasion technique, you are that certain person who have the ability to make your subject be persuaded with some stories. Suppose you are practicing persuasion on a certain person you love and want changed. You are also trustworthy to that person. When you are in a position like that, you can tell a story similar to that person's story except for the details you want changed, then you can easily make the person understand which is right and wrong, why what needs to be done and which should not be done. On the other hand, metaphors have the same ability to change or persuade any people through the metaphorical descriptions.

Set a Goal: Nothing can be done without a certain vision

or goal. A goal is a target for which a person needs to put effort and walk onward. As referred in psychology, we can easily define goal as certain desire to attend and plan. For the purpose of persuasion, it is necessary to set a certain goal according which people needs to charge forward. Persuasion is depended on the neuro linguistic fact of the goal.

Get Confident and Passionate: Become enthusiastic about your technique, products, thought, or strategy. Do not forget to show passion applying your tactics. Willpower can undoubtedly be contagious and solid for salesmanship. Confidence is the key. This can often accomplish by emotionally attaching with whatever confident factors and rewards you happen to be producing with your thoughts.

It is crucial to get dismissed up, but also important to shake it off and represent confidently. In addition to this, giving logical perspectives is also helpful when it comes to ethical head game titles and persuading persons. Preserve in your head that individuals quite frequently utilize their selections based primarily on excitement, and in the long term justify those selections utilizing rational reasons. Showing interest to both of these is usually generally your best wager.

Be Upfront and Ask Directly: Another technique is to simply ask directly for whatever it is that you want. This might mean an evening out, seeking an individual to obtain your products, or prodding them to sign up for something. If you do not converse to, you will pretty much under no circumstances, discover out! An entire great deal of conditions, individuals very easily would not actually know very well what to bring out, and providing an action, believe, or choice can come to end up being useful for everyone operating.

Practice all of the know-how explained above to have an impact on salesmanship. Know how to develop and grow into strong potential. Staying excellent with salesmanship and legal steps is normally structured with the understanding of the cosmetic foundations of salesmanship. Practice a lot to able to fluently apply them. Keeping yourself smart with knowledge of salesmanship and steps tactics, can effectively defend you against persons making an attempt to employ them adversely against you.

How To Defend Yourself From Manipulation

We are indeed human at the end of the day. It is because of this very reason that we get to dwell allot on the opinion of others in everything that we do. We always desire and adore getting validation from others so that we can subconsciously decide whether we shall be depressed. In this age of the millennial, the norm has become to just brag about their wealth on social media. A lot of these bragging are often than not the truth. This ultimately leads to one having a loose relationship with reality. Self-deception of this type can dig deep into the human spicy, that a victim of these may one day wake up and realize that their perfect world is only existent within their maids. Depression will closely follow suit. The first step to attempting to defend yourself from manipulation and persuasion is confronting the situation and taking the stance of breaking off any illusions you may have. You will not be able to proceed normally with your life. You have to be wary of the fact that you are in control of your own choices. Then make the conscious choice of seeing things for what they are. That deal, which seems too good to be true, could actually be just that... too good to be true. The other thing you should follow is to definitely trust your instincts. There are times that a lie has been told to you in the most skilled way imaginable, that you will end up believing. But you can feel an imbalance on some instinctive level between what should be, what is, and then what is being projected onto you. There may be no physical signs to show that hey, something is wrong, but you feel something is wrong. The following important thing when you ask questions is to listen to the responses. This may sound somewhat unbelievable because you'll listen to the answers. The truth is that our self-disappointment can make us choose the answers we receive. We tell ourselves that we listen, but we only pay attention to the answers we want to hear rather than to the answers we receive. You may have broken the illusions around you, but some of you are still clinging to the comfort of those illusions. The pain of confronting the situation would prevent you from listening to the real answers to your questions. Actual listening requires a certain sense of detachment, but this time around not from reality. You have to get rid of your emotions. Your detachment from our emotions would lead you to the following step, which would logically process the new information. It can complicate situations more than they already are to act irrationally. It makes your exit strategy so much difficult to let all the emotions simmer and spring to the surface. When you face the truth, the irrational part of you may want you to let it all go hell. Your rightly justified anger can inspire you to take steps to calm your emotions in the short term. But you may come to regret these actions in the long term. I'm not saying that you should deny your emotions; I'm not saying that you do not act on these emotions.

Act quickly

It's great that you have come to terms with the reality of things. But defense against these dark manipulative tactics entail so much more. While attempting to defend you from the claws of these manipulators, is often intense and exhilarating at first. This intensity of these emotions may cause one to slowly slide into denial. The more you delay in taking any action is usually what accelerates the onset of this denial, and when it happens, there are high chances that you might relapse and end up getting trapped in the same web. This can be avoided by taking action immediately you realize that someone is trying to manipulate you. This can present itself in the simplest of ways like when informing a close friend of some reality of the particular situation may be all that's needed so set in motion a series of events that will eventually lead to your freedom. You should know that the fabric of illusion is made from tougher material than glass after making the choice to act. The illusion could work its way back into your heart with your emotions in high gear by using fragments of your emotions to fix it. When a liar is caught in a lie, he or she may attempt to recruit others to enforce that lie when they feel that they are no longer holding you. A deceptive partner with whom you have recently broken things off would at this point try to use the other mutual relationships in your life to change your mind. If you want to get out of this unscathed, you will need both your logic and instincts. Although the truth of the situation is that when you discover that you've been lied to consistently, you become emotionally scarred, so the issue of leaving the situation unscathed becomes silent. Priority should be given, however, to take the route that allows you to leave this toxic situation without harming yourself further. You're all over the place emotionally. Rage, anger, hurt, and deception is the iceberg's tip. But logically, you need to think. Keep your head above the water and warn yourself.

Get help fast

When you're trapped by other people's manipulations, confusion is one of the emotions you'd experience. This helps cloud your rational thinking and leaves you feeling helpless. You might even question the reality of what you are facing at this point. It would lead to denial if you continue to entertain these doubts. You're probably going to want to conclude you've got the whole situation wrong. That you misunderstood some things and came to the wrong conclusion. Such thinking would drive back to the manipulator's arms. Resist the urge to give in by receiving a second opinion. People go to another doctor in a health crisis to get a second opinion. This is to remove any iota of doubt about the first diagnosis that you may have and to affirm the best treatment course for you.

Similarly, getting another person's opinion can help you discern the truth of the situation and what might be your following steps. Just remember, it's better to go to someone who has proved countless times they're interested in your best. The following step is to confront the perpetrator if you have the help you need. For this, I suggest you choose the scene or location. Choose a place you know that gives you the upper hand. On your part, that would require some careful planning. If the perpetrator exists in the cyber world, especially if the person swindled you of your money, you would have to involve the police and the relevant authorities. Do some of your own investigations to ascertain the truth. After you face the perpetrator and take the necessary steps to get out of the situation, you must start the healing process quickly.

The scale and gravity to which you were hurt, manipulated or abused do not matter. You must be able to walk past it and wait until you can "heal" your wounds, rather than sitting on your couch and reliving the past. If you don't do anything about it, an unhealthy scab could form over the wound, which would make you as vulnerable if not more than you had experienced. Speak to a counsellor, attend therapy, and take an active part in facilitating the healing process, whatever you choose to do. It won't happen overnight, but you are sure that you get closer to improving every day and every step you take in therapy.

Trust your instincts

While your brain interprets signals based on facts, logic, and sometimes experience, your heart works in the opposite direction by screening information through an emotional filter. The only thing that picks up vibrations is your gut instinct, which neither the heart nor the brain can pick on. And if you can groom to the point where you recognize your inner voice and are trained to react to it, you will lower your chances of being seduced by people trying to work on you with their manipulative will. To begin with, it's hard to recognize this voice. And that's because we allowed voices of doubt, self-discrimination as well as the critics loud voices within and without drowning out our authentic voice over the course of our lives. Your survival depends on this voice or instinct. So, trust that when it kicks in, your brain neurons can still process things in your immediate vicinity.

Some people call it intuition, and some refer to it as instinct, especially when it comes to relationships, they are undoubtedly the same thing. You must accept that it may not always make logical sense to start trusting your instincts. If you've ever been in the middle of doing something and experienced the feeling of being watched all of a sudden, then you know what I mean. You don't have eyes at the back of your head, there's no one else with you in the room, but you get the tiny shiver running down your spine and the "sudden knowledge" you're watching. That's what I'm talking about. The first step to connect with your instinct is to decode your mind with the voices you've let in. With meditation, you can do this. Forget the chatter of "he said, she said." Concentrate on your center. You are the voice you know. Then, be careful about your thoughts. Don't just throw away the eclectic monologs in your head. Rather go with the thoughts flow.

Why do you think of a certain person in some way? How do you feel so deeply about this person, even if you only knew each other for a few days? What's that nagging feeling about this other person that you have? You get more tuned to your intuition as you explore your thoughts and understand when your instincts kick and how to react to it. You may need to learn to take a step back to pause and think if you are the kind of person who prefers to make spur decisions at the moment. This moment in which you pause gives you the opportunity to really reflect on your decisions and evaluate them. The following part is a hard part and it couldn't be followed by many people. Unfortunately, you can't skip or navigate around this step. This part has to do with trust. You need to be open to the idea of trusting yourself and trusting others to be able to trust your instinct. Your failure to trust others would just make you paranoid, and it's not your instincts that kick when you're paranoid. It's the fear of you. Fear tends to turn every molehill into a hill. You must let go of your fear, embrace confidence, and let that lead in your new relationships. You are better able to hear the voice inside without the roadblocks put up by fear in your mind. Finally, your priorities need to be re-evaluated. If your mind is at the forefront of money and material possessions, you may not be able to see the past. Any interaction you have with people would be interpreted as people trying to take advantage of you, and if you dwell on that frequently enough, it will soon become your reality. You know how you attract into your life what you think of. If you're constantly thinking about material wealth, you're only going to attract people who think like you. Using this as a guide, look at all your relationships with this new hindsight; the old, the new, and the perspective. Don't enter a relationship that expects to be played. Be open when you approach them, whether it's a business relationship, a romantic relationship or even a regular acquaintance. You can get the right feedback about them from your intuition. Do not step into this thinking, too, that your gut will tell you to run in the opposite direction when you meet suspect people.

Conclusion

In our world, we need to start to become more aware of manipulation. When you can recognize that someone is trying to control you, it will be much easier to stay out of their controlling grasp.

When you start to better identify manipulation, how it develops, and how it has affected your life, then it will only become easier to navigate without it. Interacting with others can include doing your best to avoid it healthily. However, stopping ourselves from being manipulated isn't the only important thing we will be discussing.

We will pay significant attention to how you can become a persuasive person yourself. Though you might have been hurt in the past by manipulation, or even damaged your mental health by being the manipulator yourself, there is hope, now that we can work towards a better future for ourselves. This is done by becoming an inspirational and potentially influential person.

Manipulation is dangerous, but when it is put in a more positive light, it can become healthy influence.

If you are able to be a persuasive individual and not only get what you want, but fulfill the needs of others as well, then it will become easier for you to be able to get the things that you desire the most in life.

Rather than always doing things you don't enjoy, being the "yes man," or letting people take advantage of your good nature, you can become just as influential as the people who have tried to control you before.

You might even be at a point where you fear manipulation altogether. Why would you want to do something to others that has actually caused you grief in the past? This kind of thinking is because we have only been aware of the negative types of manipulation. Not only that, but it is important to ensure we have the tools to understand how to get these things.

The first important step in this process is to investigate the personality types of manipulators, as well as the people whom they commonly go after. You may have heard of the common personality type, "Narcissist," a person who is only concerned with himself and getting the things he wants. Narcissists might take advantage of empaths, or highly sensitive people who are more concerned with the wellbeing of others.

After that, we will further explore positive manipulative personalities and the way that you can adopt some of these helpful practices in your own relationships.

Aside from that, we will also be discovering how our bodies communicate, the signals and responses that we give off, and what others might be taking away from our body language. The better you can understand influence through ways besides our verbal communication, the easier it will be to avoid becoming influenced yourself and to better persuade those around you.

After we understand what all of this means, it will be easier to learn and practice the rest of the influential tips that we will be sharing throughout the book.

Though it might seem easier to negatively manipulate those from whom you want something, the person whom you would be hurting most in this process is going to be yourself.

Always look for ways of positive influence so that you can mutually benefit both parties.

www.ingramcontent.com/pod-product-compliance
Lightning Source LLC
Chambersburg PA
CBHW080624030426
42336CB00018B/3072